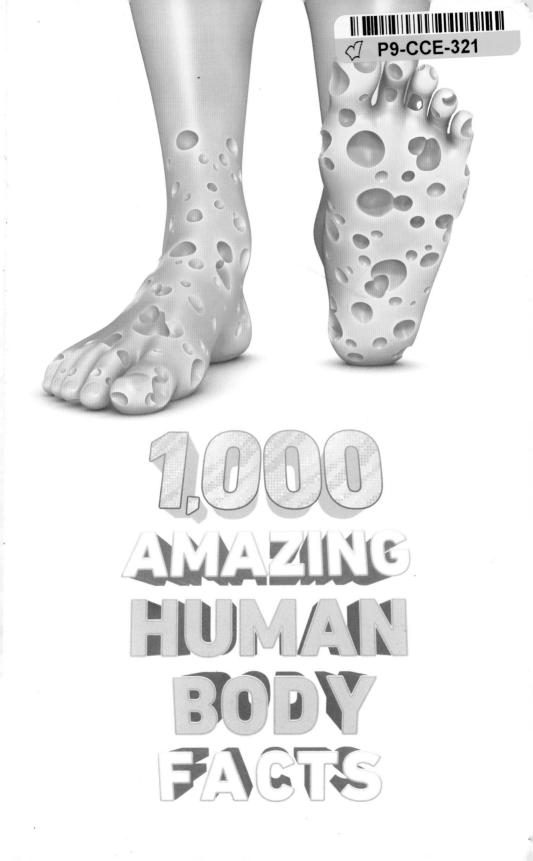

1,000
AMAZING
HUMAN
BODY
FACTS

Senior editor Ben Morgan
Senior art editor Jacqui Swan
Editors Tom Booth, Jolyon Goddard, Steve Setford
US editor Jennette ElNaggar
Designers Sunita Gahir, Laura Gardner, Lauren Quinn,
Peter Radcliffe, Samantha Richiardi, Mary Sandberg
Illustrators Adam Benton, Peter Bull,
Stuart Jackson-Carter, Arran Lewis
Creative retouching Steve Crozier
Picture research coordinator Sumita Khatwani
Jacket design Stephanie Cheng Hui Tan
Jacket design development manager Sophia MTT
Producer, pre-production George Nimmo
Senior producer Meskerem Berhane
Managing art editor Owen Peyton Jones
Managing editor Rachel Fox
Publisher Andrew Macintyre
Art director Karen Self
Associate publishing director Liz Wheeler
Publishing director Jonathan Metcalf

Writers Jolyon Goddard, Derek Harvey, Tom Jackson,
Andrea Mills, Ben Morgan, Ginny Smith, Nicola Temple

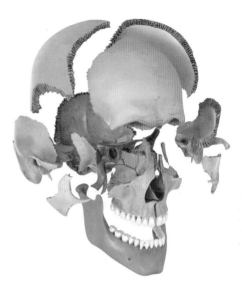

First American Edition, 2021
Published in the United States by DK Publishing
1450 Broadway, Suite 801, New York, NY 10018

Copyright © 2021 Dorling Kindersley Limited
DK, a Division of Penguin Random House LLC
21 22 23 24 25 10 9 8 7 6 5 4 3 2 1
001–319151–Aug/2021

A catalog record for this book
is available from the Library of Congress.
ISBN 978-0-7440-2884-3

DK books are available at special discounts when
purchased in bulk for sales promotions, premiums,
fund-raising, or educational use. For details, contact:
DK Publishing Special Markets,
1450 Broadway, Suite 801, New York, NY 10018
SpecialSales@dk.com

Printed and bound in China

For the curious
www.dk.com

1,000 AMAZING HUMAN BODY FACTS

CONTENTS

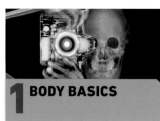

1 BODY BASICS

2 OUTER BARRIER

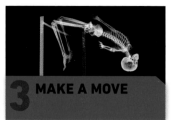

3 MAKE A MOVE

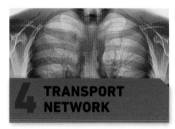

4 TRANSPORT NETWORK

5 FUELING THE BODY

6 IN CONTROL

7 SUPER SENSES

8 SELF-DEFENSE

9 THE CYCLE OF LIFE

10 YOUR OPERATING SYSTEMS

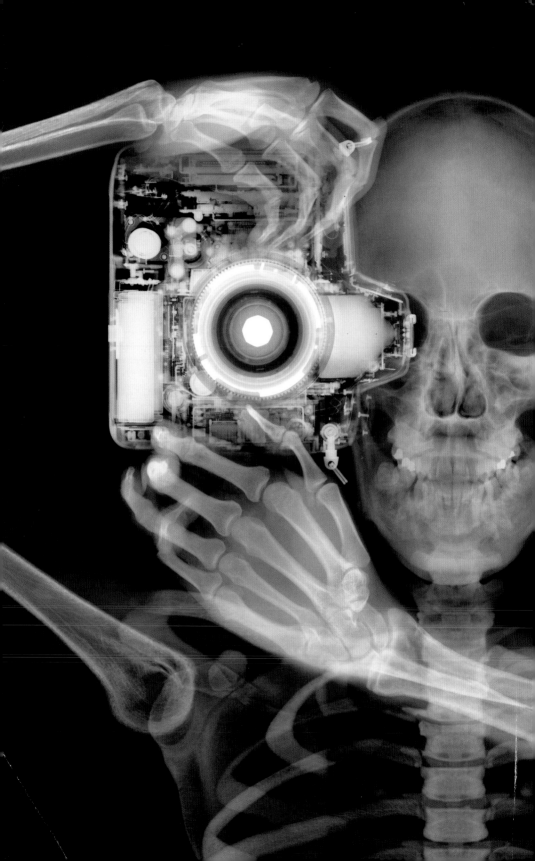

Body Basics

Your body is a giant jigsaw made of 30 trillion tiny pieces called cells. Neatly organized into tissues and organs, they work nonstop day and night to keep every part of you working.

The inside of your body is normally hidden, but an X-ray camera can see right through you to create ghostly images of your bones and teeth.

WHAT'S YOUR
BODY MADE OF?

The human body is made of exactly the same chemical substances as all other living things, from fleas to whales. The building blocks of all substances are elements—pure chemicals that can't be broken down into simpler ones. There are 118 chemical elements, but a mere six of these make up 99 percent of your body. The most abundant is oxygen, which makes up about 66 percent of your weight, and the second most abundant is carbon, which makes up 18.5 percent of your weight.

> Your body contains enough carbon to make a diamond **as big as a soccer ball.**

FAST FACTS

Your body contains a tiny amount of gold, but you'd need 40,000 people (about one full football stadium) to make a single gold ring.

There's enough iron in your body to make a 3 in (7 cm) nail. Iron is needed to carry oxygen in your blood.

Most of the elements in your body formed in the cores of dying stars.

YOUR BODY CONTAINS ABOUT 50 TEASPOONS OF SALT.

HOW IT WORKS

The four most abundant elements in the human body are oxygen, carbon, hydrogen, and nitrogen. Oxygen is the most abundant of all because it's part of water (H_2O), which makes up more than half of your weight.

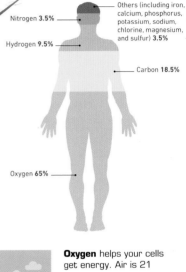

Others (including iron, calcium, phosphorus, potassium, sodium, chlorine, magnesium, and sulfur) **3.5%**

Nitrogen **3.5%**

Hydrogen **9.5%**

Carbon **18.5%**

Oxygen **65%**

Oxygen helps your cells get energy. Air is 21 percent oxygen.

Carbon is the element that diamonds and pencil lead are made from.

Hydrogen is the most common element in the universe. The sun is made of hydrogen.

Nitrogen is essential for building muscles and other tissues. Plants need it to grow.

Diamond is made of carbon atoms arranged in a crystal structure. The average person has about 27 lb (12 kg) of carbon in their body, but none of it is diamond. Instead, the carbon atoms in your body are arranged in long chains. Carbon chains form the backbones of organic molecules such as DNA, proteins, fats, and carbohydrates. All forms of life are based on carbon.

PHOSPHORUS HELPS MAKE YOUR TEETH STRONG.

YOUR BODY CONTAINS ABOUT 90 MICROGRAMS OF URANIUM.

If your cells
were as big as
grains of rice,
your body would be
the size of New York's
**Empire State
Building.**

FAST FACTS

If you laid all your 30 trillion cells end to end, you'd have enough to wrap around Earth more than 13 times.

The largest cell in the living world is the egg of an ostrich—it's about 6 in (15 cm) long.

1665
CELLS WERE **DISCOVERED** IN THE YEAR 1665.

GENES ARE STORED IN CELLS AS **DNA MOLECULES.**

HOW MANY
CELLS DO
YOU HAVE?

Your body is made up of around 30 trillion tiny, living building blocks called cells. A typical body cell is only 0.004 in (0.1 mm) wide—less than half the width of an average strand of hair—though many cells are far smaller. Some cells, such as brain cells, last your whole lifetime, but others wear out and die after a few weeks. To replace them, your body produces millions of new cells every second.

HOW IT WORKS

Living cells work like miniature factories and carry out hundreds of different tasks every second. Inside a cell are tiny structures called organelles that perform each task.

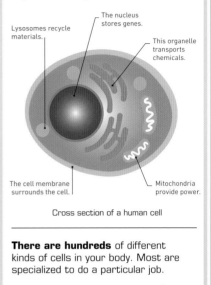

Lysosomes recycle materials.

The nucleus stores genes.

This organelle transports chemicals.

The cell membrane surrounds the cell.

Mitochondria provide power.

Cross section of a human cell

There are hundreds of different kinds of cells in your body. Most are specialized to do a particular job.

Red blood cells pick up oxygen in your lungs and carry it to cells everywhere in your body. They give blood its color.

Nerve cells carry electrical signals around your body. Your brain is made of billions of nerve cells.

Muscle cells contain parts that can shorten very quickly to produce movement.

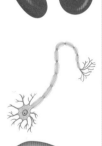

NEW CELLS ARE CREATED BY **CELL DIVISION.**

THE WORD CELL COMES FROM A LATIN WORD THAT MEANS SMALL ROOM.

What in the world?

HUMAN CELLS

Most of the cells in your body are specialized for a particular task. This electron microscope image shows the cells lining the main airway to the lungs magnified to 5,000 times their true size. These cells secrete a slimy liquid called mucus that traps particles of dirt in the air. Clusters of tiny hairs called cilia (shown here colored green) beat back and forth to push the mucus up to the throat, where it is swallowed.

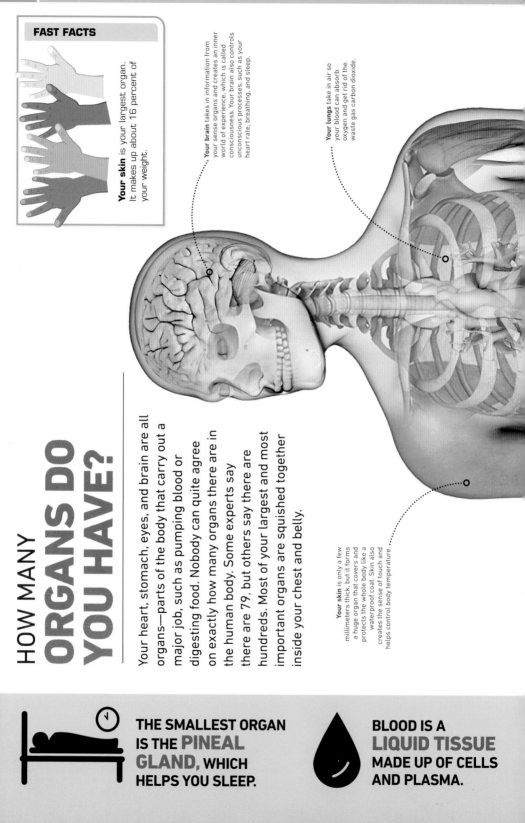

FAST FACTS

Your skin is your largest organ. It makes up about 16 percent of your weight.

Your brain takes in information from your sense organs and creates an inner world of experience, which is called consciousness. Your brain also controls unconscious processes, such as your heart rate, breathing, and sleep.

Your lungs take in air so your blood can absorb oxygen and get rid of the waste gas carbon dioxide.

Your skin is only a few millimeters thick, but it forms a huge organ that covers and protects the whole body like a waterproof coat. Skin also creates the sense of touch and helps control body temperature.

HOW MANY
ORGANS DO YOU HAVE?

Your heart, stomach, eyes, and brain are all organs—parts of the body that carry out a major job, such as pumping blood or digesting food. Nobody can quite agree on exactly how many organs there are in the human body. Some experts say there are 79, but others say there are hundreds. Most of your largest and most important organs are squished together inside your chest and belly.

THE SMALLEST ORGAN IS THE **PINEAL GLAND,** WHICH HELPS YOU SLEEP.

BLOOD IS A **LIQUID TISSUE** MADE UP OF CELLS AND PLASMA.

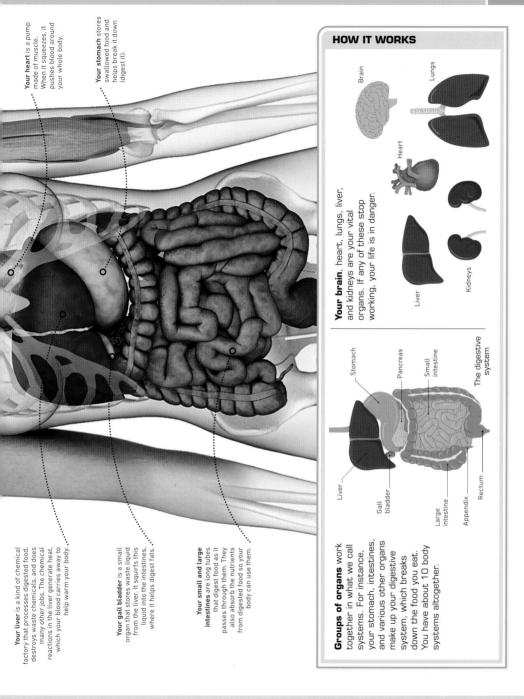

Your heart is a pump made of muscle. When it squeezes, it pushes blood around your whole body.

Your stomach stores swallowed food and helps break it down (digest it).

Your liver is a kind of chemical factory that processes digested food, destroys waste chemicals, and does many other jobs. The chemical reactions in the liver generate heat, which your blood carries away to help warm your body.

Your gall bladder is a small organ that stores waste liquid from the liver. It squirts this liquid into the intestines, where it helps digest fats.

Your small and large intestines are long tubes that digest food as it passes through them. They also absorb the nutrients from digested food so your body can use them.

HOW IT WORKS

Brain

Lungs

Heart

Liver

Kidneys

Your brain, heart, lungs, liver, and kidneys are your vital organs. If any of these stop working, your life is in danger.

Stomach

Pancreas

Small intestine

Liver

Gall bladder

Large intestine

Appendix

Rectum

The digestive system

Groups of organs work together in what we call systems. For instance, your stomach, intestines, and various other organs make up your digestive system, which breaks down the food you eat. You have about 10 body systems altogether.

A DONOR HEART CAN SURVIVE FOR **4 HOURS** BEFORE A TRANSPLANT.

A DONOR LIVER CAN SURVIVE **12 HOURS** BEFORE A TRANSPLANT.

Body Facts

SMALLER AND SMALLER

The **human body** can be *broken down into* **smaller and smaller parts,** such as **organs, cells, and molecules.** Studying the body at these different **levels of organization** helps us *understand it better.*

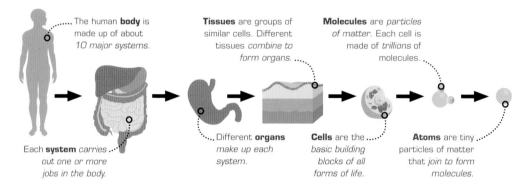

The human **body** is made up of about *10 major systems.*

Tissues are groups of similar cells. Different tissues *combine to form organs.*

Molecules are *particles of matter.* Each cell is made of *trillions of* molecules.

Each **system** *carries out one or more jobs in the body.*

Different **organs** *make up each system.*

Cells are the *basic building blocks of all forms of life.*

Atoms are tiny particles of matter that *join to form molecules.*

TRILLIONS OF CELLS

Your body is made of about **30 trillion cells** *of hundreds of different types,* but the **vast majority** of them are *blood cells.* **Blood cells** ferry *vital supplies* around your body, repair *wounds,* and help fight off *germs.*

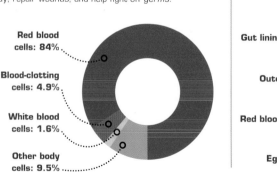

Red blood cells: 84%

Blood-clotting cells: 4.9%

White blood cells: 1.6%

Other body cells: 9.5%

HOW LONG DO CELLS LAST?

Some cells **last a lifetime,** but others *die after just a few days* and have to be **replaced.** Cells in **hardworking** parts of the body, like the lining of the intestines, have the **shortest** life spans.

Gut lining cells	3 days	10 days	Taste bud cells
Outer skin	1 month	2 months	Sperm
Red blood cells	4 months	8 years	Fat cells
Egg cells	50 years	Lifetime	Nerve cells

YOUR BODY CONTAINS THE SAME AMOUNT OF POTASSIUM AS 160 BANANAS.

ABOUT 2,000 HEART TRANSPLANTS TAKE PLACE IN THE US EVERY YEAR.

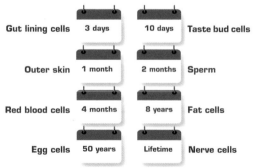

ORGAN TRANSPLANTS

Most of your **organs** *come in pairs,* which means you have a **backup** if one of them *fails.* However, **disease or injury** may make it necessary to **replace an organ** with a **transplant**. The world's *first successful* organ transplant took place in **1954** when an American man *donated a kidney to his* **identical twin brother.**

2010 First successful full face transplant

2003 First successful tongue transplant

1983 First successful lung transplant

1967 First successful heart transplant

1967 First successful liver transplant

1954 First successful kidney transplant

1998 First successful hand transplant

2008 First baby born after an ovary transplant

SEEING INSIDE

In the past, **doctors** had to *cut the human body open to* **see inside it,** but today they can use a range of different **imaging techniques.** These **technologies** have made it much easier to *diagnose and treat* disease.

ABOUT
3.6 BILLION
medical X-ray images
are made every year.

1600s First microscope

1895 X-rays discovered

1956 First medical ultrasound machine

1972 First CT scans

1998 First MRI scans

Microscopes make it possible *to see individual cells* to spot **cancer** or identify **infectious microbes** (germs).

X-rays are invisible rays that *pass through the body* but are blocked by bones and teeth. They are used to *detect* **tooth decay** and **fractures.**

Ultrasound machines use echoes of sound waves *to build up pictures of* **unborn babies** or **organs** inside the body.

CT (computed tomography) scanning combines lots of **X-ray images** on a computer to create images that show a slice through the body at any angle.

MRI (magnetic resonance imaging) picks up radio waves from **hydrogen atoms** in the body *to create images of soft body parts* that aren't visible on X-rays, such as **brain tissue.**

THERE ARE ABOUT
10 OCTILLION
ATOMS IN AN ADULT HUMAN BODY.

A CELL MAY DIVIDE 10,000 TRILLION TIMES IN YOUR LIFE.

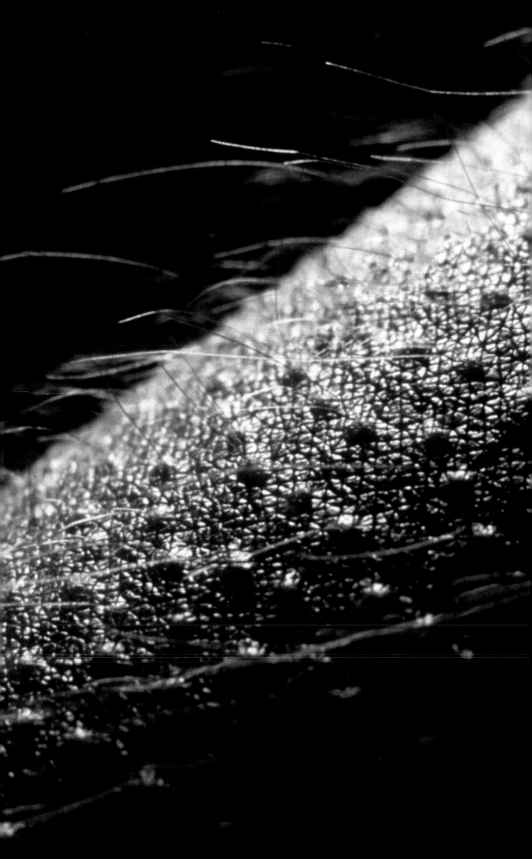

uter Barrier

Wrapped around your body like a protective overcoat, your skin forms a barrier between the inside of your body and the outside world. Your skin is waterproof, repels germs, and continually repairs and renews itself.

Goose bumps don't just happen when you're scared—they are part of your body's temperature control system. Each tiny bump is caused by a muscle that makes a hair stand up to help keep you warmer.

HOW MUCH SKIN
DO YOU GROW?

Your skin has to endure a lot of wear and tear, so to keep it in top condition, your body continually replaces it. Every second, about 30,000 dead skin cells fall off you and 30,000 new ones are made. Over the course of about a month, your whole outer layer of skin is renewed. Skin is more than just a protective outer coat. It also regulates your body temperature, gives you the sense of touch, and helps you grip and hold things.

> Your outer layer of skin regrows about **700 times** in your life.

FAST FACTS

The average person has about 19 sq ft (1.8 sq m) of skin—the same area as a single-bed sheet.

Your thinnest skin is on your eyelids and is 0.02 in (0.5 mm) thick. Your thickest skin is on the soles of your feet and is up to 0.2 in (5 mm) thick.

16%

16% OF YOUR BODY WEIGHT CONSISTS OF SKIN.

SCAR TISSUE HAS NO HAIR OR SWEAT GLANDS.

HOW IT WORKS

The top layer of your skin is called the epidermis and is less than 0.04 in (1 mm) thick. It wears off at the top but continually regrows from the bottom. New cells die after forming but then flatten and harden to form a protective wall.

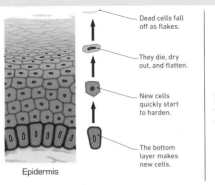

Epidermis

Dead cells fall off as flakes.

They die, dry out, and flatten.

New cells quickly start to harden.

The bottom layer makes new cells.

Fingerprints are made of tiny ridges that help your fingers grip, like the tread on a tire. Your fingerprint patterns are unique to you.

Skin has two distinct layers: a dead layer and a living layer. The top layer, the epidermis, is made of dead cells that form a tough, waterproof barrier to protect the living tissues below from injuries and invasion by germs. Under the epidermis is the dermis. This layer contains living hair roots, sweat glands, blood vessels, and nerve cells that sense touch and pain.

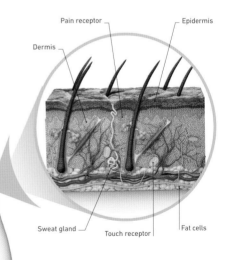

Pain receptor

Epidermis

Dermis

Sweat gland

Touch receptor

Fat cells

THE **COLOR** OF SKIN COMES FROM CELLS CALLED MELANOCYTES.

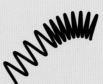

SKIN BECOMES LESS **ELASTIC** AS PEOPLE AGE.

What in the world?

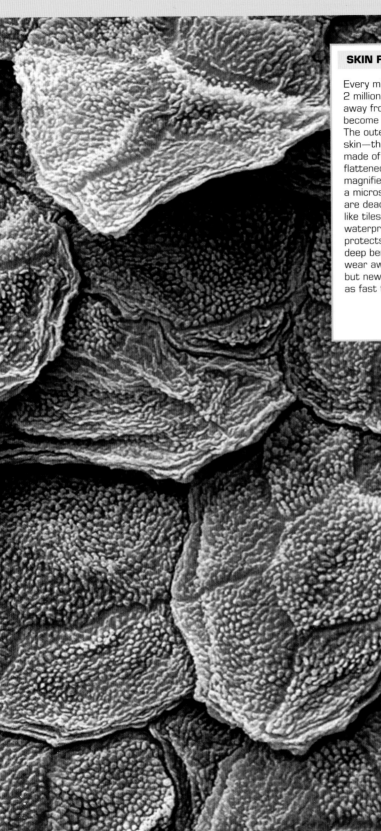

SKIN FLAKES

Every minute about
2 million dead cells flake
away from your skin to
become household dust.
The outermost layer of
skin—the epidermis—is
made of billions of tough,
flattened cells, seen here
magnified 4,000 times by
a microscope. These cells
are dead but interlock
like tiles to form a tough,
waterproof barrier that
protects the living tissue
deep beneath. Skin cells
wear away continually,
but new ones form just
as fast to replace them.

The speed at which nails grow varies from person to person, from fingers to toes, and from finger to finger. Fingernails grow up to four times faster than toenails, and nails on long fingers grow faster than those on short fingers. Exercise, diet, gender, and even the time of year all affect how quickly your nails grow.

The outer layer of an animal's skin is made of keratin—the same substance fingernails are made of.

HOW IT WORKS

The visible part of a nail is called the nail plate. This is made of dead cells hardened by a tough protein called keratin. Under the plate is the nail bed—a living layer made of special skin cells. New nail cells form in the root, hidden from view. After forming, they move forward, harden with keratin, and die. It takes about six months for cells to move from the root to the tip.

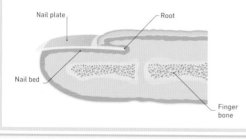

Nail plate

Root

Nail bed

Finger bone

WHEN A WOMAN IS PREGNANT, HER FINGERNAILS GROW FASTER.

MONKEYS AND **APES** AS WELL AS HUMANS HAVE FINGERNAILS.

HOW FAST DO
NAILS GROW?

Your fingernails grow by an average of 0.14 in (3.5 mm) a month, so if you never cut or chewed them, each one would reach a whopping 11 ft (3.4 m) in your life—about twice your height. Fingernails are precision tools that allow you to prize, cut, grip, tap, and scrape. Imagine trying to scratch an itch without them! They also protect the ends of your fingers and toes and enhance your sense of touch.

Your eight fingers and two thumbs produce about **110 ft (34 m)** of nail in your life— the length of **seven elephants.**

If you did manage to grow your nails really long, they would curl rather than grow straight.

FAST FACTS

Fingernails grow at about the same speed that continents drift across Earth's surface.

The world record for the longest fingernails is held by Christine Walton of the US. The total length of all her fingernails combined is 20 ft (6 m).

ONYCHOPHAGIA
MEANS BITING YOUR FINGERNAILS WHEN NERVOUS.

NAIL POLISH WAS FIRST USED IN CHINA **5,000 YEARS AGO.**

HOW MANY
HAIRS DO YOU HAVE?

Don't try to count them! There are around 100,000 hairs on your head but another 5 million or so on the rest of your body. Hairs cover nearly every bit of you. Thick "terminal" hairs grow on your scalp, keeping it warm and protecting it from sunburn. Tiny "vellus" hairs you can barely see grow all over the rest of you, except for your eyes, lips, palms, and the soles of your feet.

Head hair is called terminal hair.

Fine body hair is called vellus hair.

FAST FACTS

Red is the rarest hair color. Fewer than 1 in 50 people have it. It's most common in Ireland and Scotland.

Just like humans, monkeys and apes have completely hairless skin on their palms and soles. This makes it easier to grip branches in their forest habitats.

At rest, adults produce about 1 quart (1 liter) of sweat a day—that's enough to fill two bathtubs a year!

Humans have the same number of hairs as chimpanzees: 5 million.

HUMAN AND ANIMAL HAIR IS USED TO SOAK UP OIL SPILLS.

BLOND PEOPLE HAVE THE MOST HAIRS ON THEIR HEAD—ABOUT 130,000.

HOW IT WORKS

Hair and skin play a key role in keeping your body temperature just right. When you're too cold, goose bumps help keep you warm. When you're too hot, sweating cools you down.

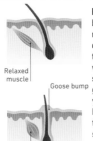

Relaxed muscle

Goose bump

Muscle pulls on base of hair

Each hair on your body has a tiny muscle that pulls on its base, making the hair stand up when you're cold or scared. This creates goose bumps on your skin. When hairs stand up, they trap more air and so help keep your skin warm.

Sweat oozes out of millions of tiny pores in your skin and cools your body as it evaporates. The skin of adults also produces an oily, smelly type of sweat when they're scared or nervous.

Normal sweat gland

Oily sweat gland

Dense, shaggy hair covers most mammals, such as chimpanzees.

Most mammals are covered in dense fur to keep them warm, but humans are an exception. Our body hairs are so fine that we look naked. That's because fur would interfere with our cooling system. Most mammals cool down by panting, but humans cool down by sweating. Sweat takes heat away from the skin as it evaporates.

HUMAN HAIR WAS FOUND IN A 257,000-YEAR-OLD HYENA POO.

ATHLETES PRODUCE UP TO 1.5 QUARTS (1.5 LITERS) OF SWEAT AN HOUR DURING EXERCISE.

About **80** percent of the world's people have dark brown or black hair.

Head hairs usually grow for 2–6 years before falling out. How long your hairs can grow depends on how long they last before falling out. Most people's hair doesn't grow much longer than their waist, but the world record is 18.5 ft (5.6 m).

FAST FACTS

All the hair you can see on your body is dead. Living cells are found only in the roots of hairs.

Hair grows faster in summer than winter.

Eyebrow hairs grow for only four months, which is why they don't need cutting.

If your hairs never fell out and were never cut, they'd grow to **seven times your height** in your lifetime.

Hair is made of a tough substance called keratin, which also forms your nails and the outer layer of skin.

IT TAKES UP TO 2 YEARS TO GROW **SHOULDER-LENGTH HAIR.**

GRAY HAIR IS A MIXTURE OF WHITE AND FULLY COLORED HAIRS.

HOW MUCH
HAIR DO YOU GROW?

You may not notice it, but each hair on your head grows by about 0.4 in (1 cm) a month. There are 100,000 or so hairs on your head, which means you grow a whopping 0.6 miles (1 km) of hair each month. In a lifetime, that adds up to a hair-rising total of 620 miles (1,000 km)—enough hair, if you laid the strands end to end, to stretch from Chicago to Washington, DC.

HOW IT WORKS

Hairs grow from tiny pits in your skin called follicles. These don't produce hair continuously—they take occasional rests, during which a new hair forms and the old one falls out. Most head hairs last only a few years and so don't normally grow longer than 3 ft (1 m).

The hair follicle makes new cells at the root. The cells harden and die, before being pushed out as a growing strand of hair.

Over time, the hair follicle gets narrower. The root eventually separates from its blood supply and the hair stops growing.

A new hair begins to grow in the base of the follicle. The old hair is pushed out.

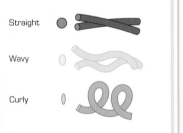

Straight

Wavy

Curly

The way your hair grows depends on the shape of your hair follicles. Round follicles produce straight hair, oval follicles produce wavy hair, and flat follicles produce curly hair.

IT TAKES UP TO 6 YEARS TO GROW HAIR DOWN TO YOUR WAIST.

UNBORN BABIES ARE COVERED IN LANUGO— FINE HAIR THAT FALLS OUT BEFORE BIRTH.

What in the world?

EYELASHES

Eyelashes protect the delicate surface of your eyes from flecks of dirt. They are highly sensitive—anything that touches them triggers a blinking reflex, closing the eyelid completely for extra protection. In this electron microscope image, the tails of tiny mites are visible at the base of the hairs. These skin-eating creatures related to spiders live harmlessly in most people's skin.

Skin, Nail, and Hair Facts

KERATIN KINGDOM

As well as forming **hair and nails** and helping **make skin tough**, the protein **keratin** is found in many other **animal body parts**.

Claws

Scales

Shells of tortoises

Rhino horns
(the horns and antlers of other animals are made of bone)

Beaks

Feathers

Hooves

Spines and quills

HAIR CHEMISTRY

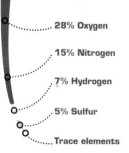

Your hair is made up of five **main elements**. There are also **small traces** of many other elements, including a minuscule amount of gold.

- **45% Carbon**
- **28% Oxygen**
- **15% Nitrogen**
- **7% Hydrogen**
- **5% Sulfur**
- **Trace elements**

There is such a **tiny amount of gold** in hair that you would need **165 tons** of hair to make a gold ring.

Growing hair can absorb chemicals from our bodies. Hairs found at crime scenes can tell **forensic scientists** whether a suspect or victim was taking **medicines or illegal drugs**.

EXTREME MAMMALS

Some mammals have many **millions more hairs** than humans, while others are **nearly hairless**.

Naked mole rats have only about **100** fine body hairs and a few more between their toes.

A sea otter's fur is super-dense. An adult can have around **900 million** hairs in all.

80% OF TEENAGERS SUFFER FROM ACNE.

TIGERS HAVE STRIPED **SKIN** AS WELL AS STRIPED **FUR.**

WORKING UP A SWEAT

People's bodies produce different amounts of **sweat** depending on how hard they work and how hot it is.

Average: **1 quart** (1 liter) per day

Moderate exercise: **6 quarts** (6 liters) per day

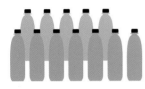

Lots of exercise in hot weather: **12 quarts** (12 liters) per day

SPOTTER'S GUIDE TO ACNE

Acne is a skin condition that produces **spots** when **skin pores become blocked** with oil and dead skin cells. *The spots can take many forms.*

Blackheads (open blocked pores)

Whiteheads (closed blocked pores)

Papules (small, red, tender bumps)

Pustules (pus-tipped papules)

Nodules (big, hard lumps under the skin)

Cysts (big, pus-filled lumps under the skin)

FINGERPRINTS

The **skin ridges on your fingertips** form unique swirly patterns. The patterns can be **arches, whorls, or loops**. When you touch things, sweat on your fingertips leaves **distinctive prints**.

Arches (about 5% of fingers have arches)

Loops (about 60% of fingers have loops)

Whorls (about 35% of fingers have whorls)

RECORDS

▲ **Toenails**
In 1991, the toenails of American **Louise Hollis** had a combined length of **7.25 ft** (2.21 m).

▲ **Tattoos**
Tattoos cover **100 percent** of the skin of New Zealander **Lucky Diamond Rich**.

▶ **Hair**
The hair of China's **Xie Qiuping** measured **18.5 ft** (5.6 m) in 2004—that's taller than the average giraffe.

▲ **Beard**
When Norwegian-American **Hans Langseth** died in 1927, his **beard** reached **17.5 ft** (5.3 m).

HIPPOS HAVE RED "SWEAT" THAT ACTS AS A **SUNSCREEN** AND AN **ANTIBIOTIC.**

YOUR FEET PRODUCE ABOUT A **GLASSFUL OF SWEAT** EACH DAY.

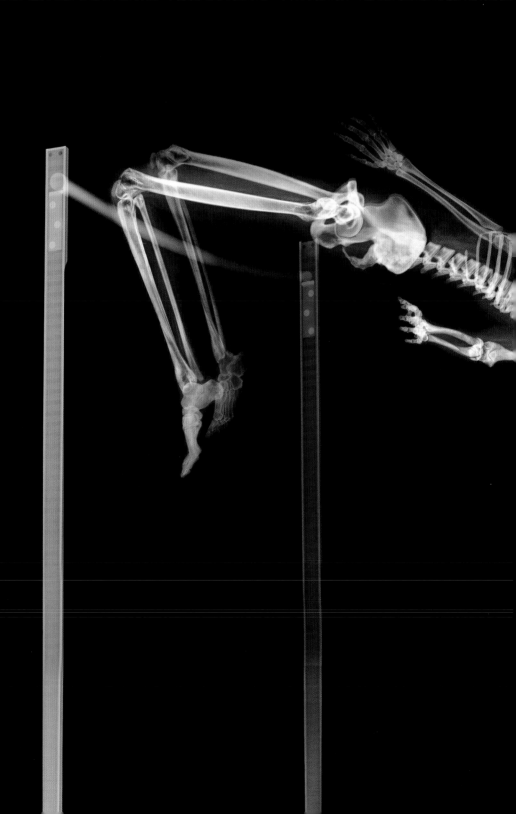

ake a Move

Bones and muscles make up about half of the weight of your body. They work together to form a living, mobile framework operated by thought alone. Skeletal muscles are also called voluntary muscles because you have complete control of what they do.

The human body is capable of incredible feats of strength and agility, but it takes training and practice to master skills as demanding as the high jump.

The number of bones in your body depends on your age. A newborn baby has about 300 bones, but some of these fuse together as the skeleton grows. By the age of 25, the human skeleton has only 206 bones.

Each arm has 30 bones, including 27 in the hand and wrist.

Your skull is made up of 22 bones. Some of them are separate in babies, but they gradually fuse during childhood.

HOW MANY
BONES DO
YOU HAVE?

Without a skeleton to hold you up, your body would collapse into a wobbling mound of flesh. Your skeleton is made of up to 300 bones, which are connected by joints and tightly wrapped with more than 600 muscles. This living framework allows you to walk, dance, climb trees, and ride bikes. It also protects your organs, stores minerals, and produces 95 percent of your blood cells.

FAST FACTS

Most large animals have an endoskeleton—a skeleton inside the body. Many small animals, however, have an exoskeleton—a skeleton on the outside.

Endoskeletons   Exoskeletons

Sharks have zero bones. Their internal skeletons are made entirely of a tough, rubbery tissue called cartilage.

THE **LARGEST** BONE EVER FOUND WAS A DINOSAUR THIGHBONE.

14%

YOUR SKELETON IS ABOUT 14% OF YOUR **WEIGHT.**

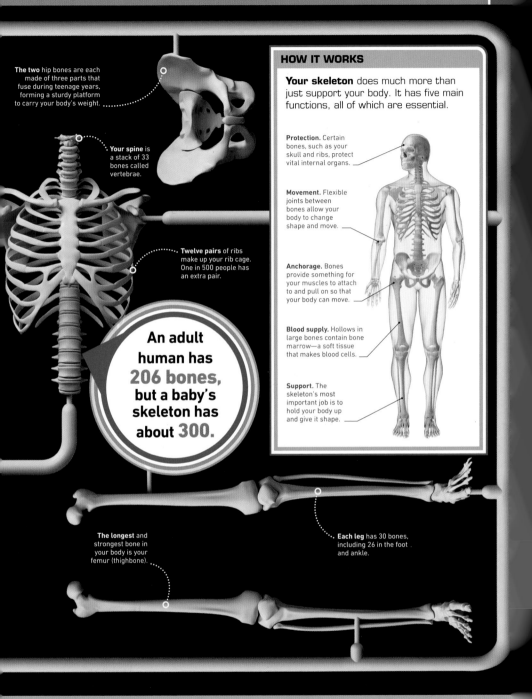

The two hip bones are each made of three parts that fuse during teenage years, forming a sturdy platform to carry your body's weight.

Your spine is a stack of 33 bones called vertebrae.

Twelve pairs of ribs make up your rib cage. One in 500 people has an extra pair.

An adult human has **206 bones,** but a baby's skeleton has about **300.**

HOW IT WORKS

Your skeleton does much more than just support your body. It has five main functions, all of which are essential.

Protection. Certain bones, such as your skull and ribs, protect vital internal organs.

Movement. Flexible joints between bones allow your body to change shape and move.

Anchorage. Bones provide something for your muscles to attach to and pull on so that your body can move.

Blood supply. Hollows in large bones contain bone marrow—a soft tissue that makes blood cells.

Support. The skeleton's most important job is to hold your body up and give it shape.

The longest and strongest bone in your body is your femur (thighbone).

Each leg has 30 bones, including 26 in the foot and ankle.

YOUR SKELETON WILL **SHRINK** BY 2 IN (5 CM) BETWEEN THE AGES OF **30 AND 70.**

SOME SNAKES HAVE MORE THAN **1,000** BONES IN THEIR SKELETON.

HOW STRONG ARE
YOUR BONES?

Gram for gram, bone is stronger than solid steel and four times stronger than concrete. The great strength of bone comes from its smart structure. A bone isn't solid all the way through; its interior has a honeycomb structure with hollows and crisscrossing struts. This makes bone lightweight but able to withstand powerful forces.

The strongest bones in your body are your thighbones (femurs), which can briefly withstand forces up to 30 times your weight. This may sound extreme, but running and jumping generate forces much greater than your weight. Long bones like your femurs can withstand these forces when squeezed from end to end, but a sudden force from the side can bend them and cause them to fracture.

Seen through a microscope, the inside of a large bone looks like a sponge. The hollows keep bones lightweight.

Four human thighbones can support a 7 ton truck.

YOUR BONES REACH
PEAK **STRENGTH**
WHEN YOU'RE
ABOUT AGE **30.**

ASTRONAUTS IN
SPACE LOSE UP TO
2% OF THEIR BONE
STRENGTH A MONTH.

HOW IT WORKS

A typical bone has a number of layers. The strongest part is the outer layer, called compact bone. This is packed almost solid with the mineral calcium phosphate—the substance that makes teeth hard. Deeper inside is spongy bone, which has hollows to reduce weight. Large bones also have a hollow center containing a soft tissue called bone marrow.

Compact bone

Spongy bone

Bone marrow

FAST FACTS

The strongest bone in the world may be the thighbone of a rhinoceros. It can support an estimated 110 tons.

Nearly a third of the weight of bone consists of fibers of collagen—an elastic (stretchy) kind of protein. These fibers are embedded in the hard parts of bones and make them slightly springy, which helps them resist breaking.

MOST BIRDS HAVE HOLLOW BONES TO REDUCE WEIGHT AND HELP THEM FLY.

PENGUINS HAVE SOLID BONES TO INCREASE WEIGHT AND HELP THEM DIVE.

What in the world?

BONE CELLS

Even the hardest parts
of bones are not entirely
solid. They are riddled
with tiny cavities (the
black specks in this
microscope image) that
each contain a living bone
cell. Bone cells continually
repair and remodel the
solid bone around them.
If you exercise, they make
your bones stronger. They
build up layers of hard,
crystalline minerals in
concentric cylinders,
like rings in a tree trunk.
This gives bones great
strength but also a
degree of flexibility.

HOW MANY
BONES ARE IN
YOUR SKULL?

Your skull acts like a built-in helmet that protects your brain from injuries. It consists of a jigsaw of bones held together by joints that can't move. One exception, however, is your mandible, or jawbone, which moves whenever you speak or eat. As well as protecting your brain, your skull provides a home for your main sense organs: your ears, eyes, mouth, and nose.

FAST FACTS

Babies' skulls have several large gaps that are filled with soft tissue. These gaps, called fontanelles, make the skull bendy enough to squish a little during birth. That's why newborn babies sometimes have slightly pointy heads.

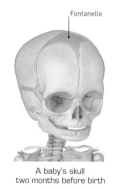

Fontanelle

A baby's skull
two months before birth

The rounded top part of the skull is called the cranium (braincase) and encloses your brain. It's made of eight plates of bone knitted together by wiggly joints to form a rigid dome. The bony parts of your face—including your eye sockets, nose, and mouth—consist of 14 bones. Most of the facial bones come in pairs, one on each side of the head.

There are 22 **bones** in the skull, but only one, the **jawbone,** can move.

THE WALLS OF SKULL CHAPEL IN KUDOWA, POLAND, ARE LINED WITH 3,000 SKULLS.

MOST OF YOUR NOSE IS MADE NOT OF BONE BUT CARTILAGE, A SOFT, RUBBERY TISSUE.

The left and right parietal bones are the largest bones in the cranium (braincase) and form its roof.

The frontal bone forms your forehead.

The temporal bone has a hole for your ear canal.

The scientific term for the cheekbone is the zygomatic bone.

Your mandible moves down to open the mouth and up to bite.

HOW IT WORKS

Compare a human skull to that of our closest ape relatives and you notice something odd. Like most mammals, apes have a long snout with a small braincase behind it, but we have a flat face, a towering forehead, and a huge, balloonlike braincase. The reason for the difference lies in our brains, which have tripled in size during the last 3 million years of human evolution. Larger brains gave our ancestors special skills that helped them survive, such as language and the ability to invent tools.

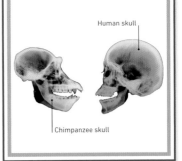

Human skull

Chimpanzee skull

THE MOST COMMON FACIAL FRACTURE IS A BROKEN NOSE.

THE DINOSAUR PENTACERATOPS HAD THE BIGGEST SKULL OF ANY LAND ANIMAL.

HOW MANY BONES ARE
IN YOUR HANDS
AND FEET?

The ends of your arms are very handy! Hands are the ultimate multipurpose tools, used to push and pull, lift and hold, grasp and manipulate. Your feet, however, only have to do one thing really well: keep you upright. Doing these jobs involves a lot of bones—27 in each hand and 26 in each foot. That's 106 bones altogether, which is more than all your other bones combined.

HOW IT WORKS

Pinch your thumb together with the tip of each finger. Only humans can do this. It's a unique ability that allows you to handle objects with more skill than any other animal. Your special thumbs allow you to grip objects in two main ways.

The power grip is used to grasp an object tightly, with your fingers and thumb wrapped around it. You use this grip to climb, throw balls, and hold heavy objects.

The precision grip is used to hold small objects between the tips of one or more fingers and the thumb. It isn't as strong as the power grip, but it's useful for fiddly tasks like tying shoelaces and writing.

Your foot bones are arranged in much the same way as your hand bones. However, foot bones are thicker to support your weight, and toe bones are shorter than finger bones as they never need to grasp things.

More than **half of the bones** in the human skeleton are in the hands and feet.

THE HANDS OF ROBERT LUDLOW OF THE US WERE A RECORD-BREAKING **12.75 IN** (32.4 CM) LONG.

THE SCIENTIFIC NAME FOR THE BIG TOE IS THE **HALLUX.**

Each toe is made of three small bones called phalanges (except the big toe, which has two). These make the toes flexible.

FAST FACTS

When you walk, the front and back parts of your feet take your weight and the middle barely presses on the ground. This is because feet have an arched shape to absorb shocks and to make them springy, which helps you run.

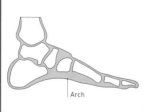

Arch

Five long bones called metatarsals form the middle part of the foot. They help make your feet springy as you walk.

The heel bone is the largest and strongest bone in your foot. When you walk or run, this bone takes all your weight as you put each foot down.

KOALAS HAVE **TWO THUMBS** ON EACH HAND TO GIVE THEM A STRONG GRIP.

A BAT'S WINGS ARE MADE OF SKIN STRETCHED OVER **FINGER BONES.**

HOW DO YOUR
BONES HEAL?

Bones are made of tough stuff, but if they're twisted, bent, or struck with too much force, they fracture. Fortunately, like most parts of your body, your bones are made of living tissue that can mend itself. The process of healing begins right after you break a bone. Special cells hidden inside every bone spring into life and multiply quickly to form a makeshift repair. Over the following months, this is remodeled and strengthened until the bone is as good as new.

It can take **a year or more** for a broken bone to **heal perfectly** and regain its full strength.

This metal plate screwed into a broken arm bone keeps the fragments still until they fuse back together.

The screws and plate are made of a metal that does not rust.

FAST FACTS

Broken bones can be very painful, but the pain is good for you. Pain makes you keep an injured part of the body still while it heals.

When doctors treat fractures, they sometimes have to realign the broken parts before the bone heals. This ensures the bone will regain its normal shape.

ON AVERAGE, A PERSON **BREAKS** 2 BONES DURING THEIR LIFE.

SMOKING MAKES BROKEN BONES HEAL MORE SLOWLY.

It's important to keep a broken bone still while it mends. This is often done by wrapping the injury with a plaster cast, but in severe cases, surgeons use metal plates and screws to hold the broken parts in place.

HOW IT WORKS

Within a few hours of a fracture, blood fills the break and forms a solid clot. The area around the bone becomes swollen and sore.

Clotted blood

After a week, the clot has been replaced by a tough, rubbery tissue called cartilage. This forms a temporary bridge across the break, but it is not as solid as bone.

The clot is replaced by cartilage.

After a month or two, struts of bone have grown through the cartilage, knitting the fragments together strongly. It is now safe to remove a plaster cast.

New bone tissue

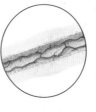

Over a year or so, bone cells remodel the area by absorbing the struts of bone and laying down new, more solid bone. The bone returns to its previous shape.

STRESS FRACTURES ARE TINY FRACTURES CAUSED BY TOO MUCH EXERCISE.

SUNLIGHT HELPS YOUR BODY MAKE VITAMIN D, WHICH KEEPS BONES STRONG

HOW DO YOUR
JOINTS WORK?

f your skeleton didn't have mobile joints, your body would be frozen still like a statue. Joints are the meeting points between bones. Like a hinge on a door, a joint holds two solid parts together but allows them to swing separately. There are hundreds of joints in your skeleton, and many work like the moving parts in a machine. Your elbows are hinges, for instance, but your shoulders are ball-and-socket joints that work like the thumbsticks in a game controller.

Condyloid joints work like ball-and-socket joints but are not as round. They allow a wide range of movement but limited rotation.

Ball-and-socket joints in your shoulders and hips allow your arms and legs to move freely in any direction.

HOW IT WORKS

Just like the moving parts in a machine, joints need lubrication to keep them working smoothly. Mobile joints are held in a watertight capsule filled with a slippery fluid that allows the bones to move past each other without scraping. The ends of the bones are coated in a smooth substance called articular cartilage. To stop the bones from pulling apart, there are ligaments—bands of very tough, fibrous tissue—that hold them together.

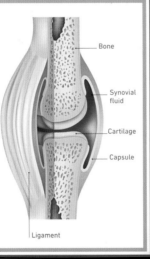

Bone

Synovial fluid

Cartilage

Capsule

Ligament

Between the bones of your spine are small cushions of shock-absorbing tissue. These hold the bones together but allow a little movement, enabling you to bend your neck and back.

THE ROOTS OF TEETH ARE ANCHORED TO BONES BY RIGID JOINTS.

900

THERE ARE AROUND 900 LIGAMENTS IN THE BODY.

Different kinds of joints allow different movements. Some joints are cleverly shaped to allow free movement in only certain directions. Others, such as those in your skull, are rigid and so allow no movement whatsoever.

Rigid joints in your skull glue different bones firmly together, allowing no movement.

Saddle joints allow bending in many directions but prevent twisting.

A pivot joint works like a steering wheel. The one in the top of your neck allows you to turn your head from side to side.

Hinge joints in your elbows allow your lower arm to bend in only one direction. You also have hinge joints in your knees, ankles, and fingers.

FAST FACTS

The ends of the bones in flexible joints are coated with articular cartilage. This tissue is incredibly smooth and is at least twice as slippery as ice. However, it cannot repair itself, so if it wears out, the joint is permanently damaged.

About 1 in 10 people have "hypermobile" joints. These have unusually stretchy ligaments that allow people to bend their bodies into shapes that look impossible.

THE **LARGEST** LIGAMENT IN THE ANIMAL WORLD RUNS UP A GIRAFFE'S **NECK.**

THE ANCIENT GAME OF JACKS WAS ONCE PLAYED WITH SHEEP **ANKLE BONES.**

HOW MANY
MUSCLES ARE
IN YOUR FINGERS?

Your fingers and thumbs are the most nimble parts of your body, able to master an endless range of tasks, from playing the guitar to picking your nose. The surprising thing is that they do this by remote control. Fingers and thumbs have no muscles of their own—instead, there are muscles in your arm that pull on them with cords called tendons, like strings working a puppet. Wiggle your fingers and you'll see the tendons moving in the back of your hand.

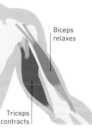

Tendons run along the tops and the bottoms of your fingers, connecting your finger bones to muscles in your forearm. When the top tendons pull, the fingers straighten. When the bottom ones pull, the fingers bend.

HOW IT WORKS

Muscles work by contracting (shortening) and pulling on bones using tendons. They usually work in pairs. For instance, you bend your arm with a muscle called the biceps, which is in the top of your upper arm, but you straighten it with a muscle on the opposite side of the arm—the triceps.

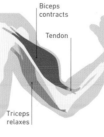

Biceps contracts

Tendon

Triceps relaxes

Biceps relaxes

Triceps contracts

THE MIDDLE FINGER IS ALWAYS THE LONGEST AND THICKEST.

YOUR FINGERPRINTS DEVELOPED ABOUT 4 MONTHS BEFORE YOU WERE BORN.

There are **zero muscles** in your **fingers and thumbs.**

Wrapped around your wrist like a watch strap is a tough sheath of tissue that keeps tendons in place.

Each thumb is controlled by nine different muscles.

Your ring finger moves with your middle finger because they are linked to the same arm muscle.

The muscles in your palms move your fingers sideways.

FAST FACTS

The strongest tendon in your body is your Achilles tendon, which attaches your calf muscle to your heel. It's slightly elastic, which adds a spring to your step as you run.

Achilles tendon

Muscles are very good at generating heat—most of the heat your body produces comes from muscle cells contracting. When you're cold, muscles generate extra heat by shivering.

THE SOUND OF FINGERS **SNAPPING** COMES FROM A FINGERTIP HITTING THE PALM.

FINGERS HAVE **THREE BONES** EACH BUT THUMBS HAVE ONLY **TWO.**

MUSCLE CELLS

The red fibers in this electron microscope image are muscle cells. These elongated cells can reach several centimeters in length and are packed together in tight bundles. Inside them are thousands of long, chainlike protein molecules that can interweave and slide past each other in an instant, making the whole muscle cell shorten. This contraction is what moves the human body.

What in the world?

Skeleton and Muscle Facts

SPINE DATA

The **spine**, or **backbone**, is made up of a lot of individual bones called **vertebrae**. Between the vertebrae are discs of slightly squishy **cartilage** that act as *shock absorbers*.

The adult spine involves ...
26 vertebrae
100 joints
More than 120 muscles
About 220 ligaments

You have 33 vertebrae at birth, but some of the lower ones fuse as you grow, leaving 26 as an adult.

MOST
EXPENSIVE BONES

The costliest **dinosaur bones** in history belong to a *Tyrannosaurus rex* known as **Stan**. They sold at auction for an amazing **$31.8 million** in 2020.

$31,800,000

Stan is about 40 ft (12 m) long and 13 ft (4 m) high.

SPACE
CHANGES

The **weightless** conditions of space can *take their toll* on **astronauts' bodies**. When the body doesn't have to work hard against **Earth's gravity**, bones become *less dense* and muscles *waste away*.

Bones: –10%
Orbiting astronauts can lose **10 percent** of their *bone mass* in **six months**. It can take **four years** to *build up* the bones again **back on Earth**.

Muscles: –20%
A space mission lasting **5–11 days** can result in a **20 percent** loss of *muscle mass*.

Muscles shrink.

Bones become less dense and more brittle.

The spine becomes longer.

Height: +3%
Astronauts can be up to **3 percent** taller while in space. The lack of gravity allows the **cartilage discs** in the spine to expand, so *the spine lengthens*.

Exercise: +2.5 h
To stop **muscles and bones** *from deteriorating*, astronauts on the International Space Station *must exercise* for **2.5 hours** each day.

90% MUSCLE MAKES UP 90% OF AN OCTOPUS'S BODY.

PEOPLE WHO WIGGLE THEIR **EARS** USE THE **AURICULAR** MUSCLES OF THE HEAD.

MUSCLE
MARVELS

All your body's muscles *perform vital tasks*, but some stand out because of their **power**, **size**, or **tireless work rate**. Here are some of the muscles with the *biggest claims to fame*.

▶ Largest
The biggest muscle is the **gluteus maximus** in your bottom. It straightens the **hip** and keeps you upright.

Gluteus maximus

▶ Strongest
The strongest muscle for its size is the **masseter**, the most powerful of your *chewing muscles*. The masseter closes the **jaw**.

Masseter
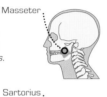

▶ Longest
At up to **23 in** (60 cm) long, the **sartorius** is the longest muscle. It runs *diagonally down* the **thigh** to the inside of the **knee**.

Sartorius

▶ Hardest working
The workhorse of the muscle world is the **heart**. It *starts beating* when you're in the **womb** and *carries on nonstop* until the day you **die**.

Heart

▶ Most active
Your busiest muscles are the ones that **move the eyes**. They move **100,000 times** a day (including at night *while you're asleep*).

Eye muscle

▶ Smallest
Connected to the tiny **stapes** bone in your *middle ear*, the **stapedius** is your smallest muscle. It is just over **0.04 in** (1 mm) in length.

Stapedius

SKELETONS AND BODY WEIGHT

The **skeletons** of larger creatures tend to make up a *higher proportion* of the animal's **body weight**. That's because *big animals need stronger bones* to support their **heavier bodies**.

Shrew 5%

Rabbit 8%

Human 14%

Elephant 20%

Skeletons as a percentage of body weight

JOURNEY OF A LIFETIME

Thanks to your **skeleton and muscles**, you can *go places*. If you live to be **80 years old**, your feet will have taken about **220 million** steps, carrying you **110,000 miles** (177,000 km). That's like walking more than four times around the world.

CRACKING STUFF

Scientists aren't sure why **knuckles and finger joints** make a **cracking** sound. It may be due to *gas bubbles forming* in **synovial fluid** of the joints—and then **popping**.

THE THREE TINY EAR BONES WOULD FIT ONTO A **PENNY** COIN.

17 YOUR **SHOULDER BLADE BONE** IS ATTACHED TO 17 MUSCLES.

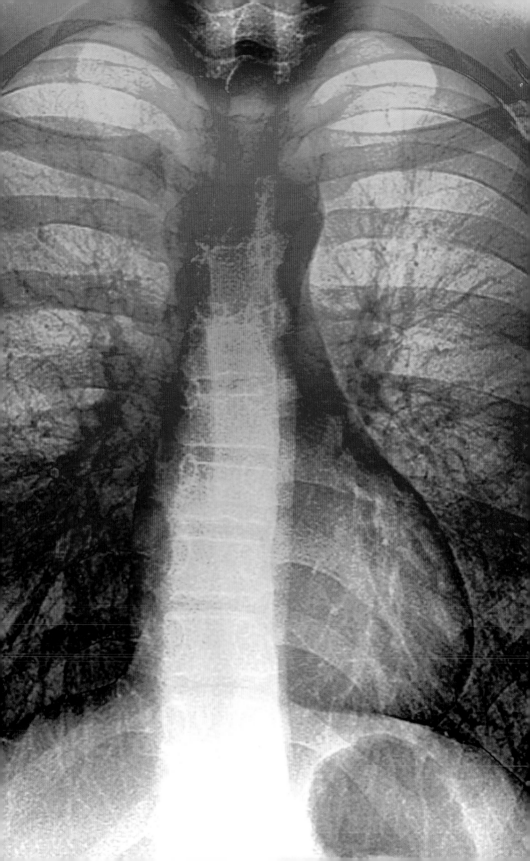

Transport Network

Every day, your heart beats about 100,000 times, its powerful muscle contracting with each beat to pump blood around your body. Your heart and blood make up your body's circulatory system—a vital transport network that keeps all your cells alive.

The heart and lungs completely fill the space inside a person's rib cage. Barely visible in this chest X-ray, the soft tissue of the lungs (blue) looks like a hollow space. The large bulge at the bottom is the heart.

Your blood vessels are long enough to wrap around **North and South America.**

HOW IT WORKS

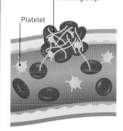

Artery Vein Capillary

There are three types of blood vessels.
Arteries are thick-walled vessels that carry blood from your heart to your tissues. Veins are thin-walled vessels that take blood back to the heart. Between them are capillaries—tiny vessels that reach nearly every cell in your body.

The clot makes bleeding stop.

Platelet

If you cut yourself, tiny cells called blood platelets clump together and trigger the formation of a net of fibers that traps blood cells. The trapped cells form a solid clot that plugs the wound.

VEINS HAVE VALVES TO STOP BLOOD FROM FLOWING BACKWARD.

BLOOD VESSELS IN YOUR FACE EXPAND AND REDDEN THE SKIN WHEN YOU BLUSH.

Laid end to end, your blood vessels could wrap around North and South America once or encircle Earth's equator 2.5 times. Most of this vast distance is made up of teeny tiny blood vessels called capillaries, which are barely wider than a single blood cell.

HOW LONG
ARE YOUR BLOOD VESSELS?

The world's longest transport system is inside you! Your network of blood vessels stretches a mind-boggling 62,000 miles (100,000 km) around your body. The busy bloodstream flows through this endless maze of tubes, delivering oxygen, nutrients, and other essential supplies to every cell in the body and carrying away waste. This vast delivery network is called your circulatory system.

Your blood gets its color from trillions of tiny, disc-shaped cells packed with a bright red chemical that carries oxygen.

FAST FACTS

Octopuses have blue blood. Instead of carrying oxygen with iron, which is what makes our blood red, octopuses use copper, which makes their blood blue.

The largest blood vessel in humans or animals is the aorta. A blue whale's aorta is so wide you could fit your head in it.

The only living part of your body that has no blood vessels is your cornea—the front part of your eye.

YOU CAN FEEL BLOOD **PUMPING** THROUGH YOUR BODY BY PRESSING ON YOUR WRIST.

BLOOD VESSELS IN YOUR SKIN **NARROW** WHEN IT'S COLD TO PREVENT **HEAT LOSS.**

HOW SMALL ARE
BLOOD CELLS?

Blood is a liquid tissue made of incredibly tiny cells floating in liquid. A red blood cell is less than a hundredth of a millimeter wide—you'd need 5,000 of them to cover this period. Your blood cells carry oxygen around your body and need to be tiny to squeeze through the narrowest blood vessels, which are finer than hairs. Blood cells contain about two-thirds of your body's iron. The iron atoms bind to oxygen molecules from air in the lungs and then release the oxygen elsewhere in your body, keeping you alive.

A 0.04 in (1 mm) cube of blood contains **5 million** red blood cells.

A RED BLOOD CELL IS ABOUT **0.0003 IN** (0.008 MM) WIDE.

ABOUT 7% OF YOUR BODY WEIGHT IS BLOOD.

Red blood cells are the most numerous cells in the human body. You have about 25 trillion of them, making up 84 percent of your cells. They are shaped like doughnuts without a hole. This roundish shape helps them flow without sticking together.

0.04 in

0.04 in

HOW IT WORKS

Your blood is made up of four ingredients: red blood cells, white blood cells, platelets, and plasma.

Red blood cells are packed with a red substance called hemoglobin, which gives blood its color. Each hemoglobin molecule contains four iron atoms that can bind to oxygen.

White blood cell

White blood cells search for invading germs, which they attack and destroy.

Platelets are tiny cells that help heal wounds by making blood clot.

Platelet

Plasma is a yellow liquid containing thousands of dissolved substances, including food molecules that provide your body with energy.

Plasma

Red marrow is a tissue inside hollow bones that makes new red blood cells. Every second, your bone marrow makes 2.4 million new red blood cells, and the same number of old, worn out cells are broken down and recycled.

115

RED BLOOD CELLS LIVE FOR AN AVERAGE OF 115 DAYS.

RED BLOOD CELLS HAVE NO DNA.

HOW MUCH BLOOD
DOES YOUR
HEART PUMP?

Your heart is the powerhouse of your body. This muscular organ constantly pumps blood around every bit of you, from head to toe. Unlike other kinds of muscles, heart muscle works nonstop without tiring or taking a break. Your heart beats about once a second for every day of your life, clocking up about 3 billion beats in a lifetime.

> Your heart pumps enough blood in your lifetime to **fill a supertanker.**

FAST FACTS

A turtle's heart can keep beating hours after the turtle dies. Nerve cells in the heart keep stimulating the muscle until it runs out of energy.

An octopus has three hearts. One pumps blood around the body and the other two pump blood to the gills.

Jellyfish have no hearts. They have no brains either. These simple animals are about 95 percent water.

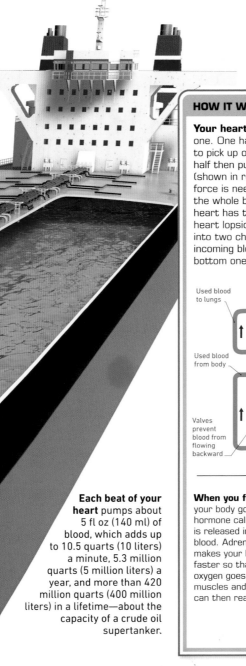

HOW IT WORKS

Your heart is actually two pumps in one. One half pumps blood to the lungs to pick up oxygen from air. The other half then pumps oxygen-rich blood (shown in red) around the body. More force is needed to send blood around the whole body, so one side of the heart has thicker muscle, making the heart lopsided. Both sides are divided into two chambers: a top one for incoming blood and a more muscular bottom one to pump it out.

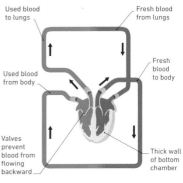

Used blood to lungs

Fresh blood from lungs

Used blood from body

Fresh blood to body

Valves prevent blood from flowing backward

Thick wall of bottom chamber

Each beat of your heart pumps about 5 fl oz (140 ml) of blood, which adds up to 10.5 quarts (10 liters) a minute, 5.3 million quarts (5 million liters) a year, and more than 420 million quarts (400 million liters) in a lifetime—about the capacity of a crude oil supertanker.

When you feel scared or excited, your body goes on high alert and a hormone called adrenaline is released into your blood. Adrenaline makes your heart beat faster so that more oxygen goes to your muscles and brain. You can then react quickly.

A BLUE WHALE'S **HEART** IS THE SIZE OF A **SMALL CAR.**

LIVING IN SPACE MAKES YOUR HEART BECOME **ROUNDER.**

FAST FACTS

If all the passages in your lungs were laid end to end, they would measure about 1,500 miles (2,400 km)— enough to stretch nearly a quarter of the way around the moon.

The airways in your lungs produce about 2 quarts (2 liters) of a slimy liquid called mucus every day. Mucus traps dust you breathe in and contains natural antibiotics that fight bacteria.

HOW BIG ARE
YOUR LUNGS?

Every cell in your body needs oxygen. Your lungs—two spongelike organs that nearly fill your chest—bring oxygen into your body each time you breathe in, as well as get rid of the waste gas carbon dioxide when you breathe out. Air travels down a network of hollow passages inside each lung until it reaches millions of tiny air pockets where oxygen is absorbed into the bloodstream.

YOUR LUNGS ARE THE ONLY ORGANS IN YOUR BODY THAT COULD FLOAT.

YOUR LEFT LUNG IS SMALLER THAN YOUR RIGHT TO MAKE ROOM FOR YOUR HEART.

The tiny air pockets in your lungs are called alveoli. Each one is smaller than a grain of sand, but because there are about 300 million in each lung, together they cover an incredible 1,000 sq ft (100 sq m) of surface area. This huge surface area allows your lungs to exchange gases quickly.

HOW IT WORKS

Air reaches your lungs through a tube called the trachea (windpipe). This main airway divides over and over again, like a tree trunk splitting into ever thinner branches and twigs, before reaching the alveoli.

Alveoli are surrounded by thin-walled blood vessels. Your blood can pick up oxygen from the air here. Your blood also releases carbon dioxide for you to breathe out. Blood cells then deliver the oxygen to the rest of your body.

Alveolus

Oxygen moves from the alveoli to the blood.

Carbon dioxide moves from the blood to the alveoli.

A **badminton** court has an area of 860 sq ft (82 sq m).

The total surface area of the air pockets in your lungs is greater than a **badminton court.**

LUNGFISH CAN BREATHE AIR AND **SURVIVE** OUT OF WATER FOR MONTHS.

YOUR LUNGS START WORKING FOR THE **FIRST TIME** JUST AFTER YOU'RE BORN.

HOW MUCH AIR
DO YOU BREATHE?

You breathe about 12 times a minute when you aren't physically active, which is more than 6 million breaths a year. You don't have to remember to breathe—it happens automatically, controlled by the bottom part of your brain (your brain stem). When you're active, your brain stem senses the need for more oxygen and makes you breathe faster and deeper. A fright or a surprise also triggers your brain stem and makes you gasp, which prepares your body for action.

> You breathe out enough air in your lifetime to fill more than **100 hot-air balloons.**

FAST FACTS

Astronauts on the International Space Station recycle their pee to make drinking water and oxygen to breathe.

In free-diving competitions, divers compete to see how far they can swim underwater while holding their breath. The world record is 663 ft (202 m).

Regular singing can increase the amount of air you're able to breathe in.

24 MINUTES & 3 SECONDS THE **LONGEST** ANYONE HAS HELD THEIR BREATH **UNDERWATER**.

WHALES BREATHE AIR THROUGH **BLOWHOLES** (NOSTRILS ON TOP OF THEIR HEADS).

A typical hot-air balloon contains about 2 million quarts (2 million liters) of air.

HOW IT WORKS

Breathing is controlled by muscles that make your chest larger and then smaller, sucking air into your lungs and then pushing it out. Under your lungs is an arched sheet of muscle called the diaphragm. When this contracts, it pulls flat and makes your lungs suck in air. At the same time, muscles between your ribs lift your rib cage and make it wider. When your diaphragm and rib muscles relax, the opposite happens: your lungs get smaller and push air out.

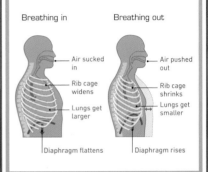

Breathing in

- Air sucked in
- Rib cage widens
- Lungs get larger
- Diaphragm flattens

Breathing out

- Air pushed out
- Rib cage shrinks
- Lungs get smaller
- Diaphragm rises

With each breath you take in about half a liter (1 pint) of air. This adds up to 6 quarts (6 liters) a minute, 9,500 quarts (9,000 liters) a day, and about 275 million quarts (260 million liters) in your life. And that's just when you're resting! If you lead a very active life, you might breathe in almost twice as much air.

HUMMINGBIRDS TAKE AN AVERAGE OF **250 BREATHS** PER MINUTE.

25 SEXTILLION THE NUMBER OF **OXYGEN MOLECULES** IN AN AVERAGE BREATH.

Heart, Blood, and Lungs Facts

HOW MUCH BLOOD DO YOU HAVE?

Your blood makes up only **7 percent** *of your weight*, but it does a lot of **important jobs**, such as *transporting* vital raw materials around your body, removing waste, and *fighting disease*. The amount of blood you have depends on your age.

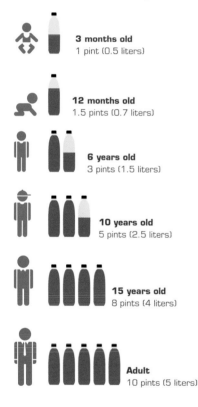

3 months old
1 pint (0.5 liters)

12 months old
1.5 pints (0.7 liters)

6 years old
3 pints (1.5 liters)

10 years old
5 pints (2.5 liters)

15 years old
8 pints (4 liters)

Adult
10 pints (5 liters)

HOW FAST DOES YOUR BLOOD FLOW?

Blood flows **fastest** as it leaves your heart and passes through the **widest blood vessels**. It slows to *less than a tenth of the speed of a garden snail* as it oozes through **blood capillaries**, then *speeds up again* as it returns to veins.

Artery: 0.9 mph (1.4 km/h)

Capillary: 0.002 mph (0.003 km/h)

Vein: 0.2 mph (0.36 km/h)

IN A HEARTBEAT

A heartbeat has **three main stages** as blood moves into and out of the heart's **top and bottom chambers**. The *dub-dub* sound of a heartbeat is caused by two sets of **valves** *closing in quick succession*.

1. Between heartbeats, the heart's muscle *relaxes* and the **heart** *fills with blood* from the body.

Blood enters the top first

Valve

2. The top chambers (atria) *contract*, their muscular walls *squeezing to push blood into* the **bottom chambers**.

Top chamber contracts

Bottom chamber fills

3. The bottom chambers (ventricles) *then contract with far more power,* pumping blood through the whole body.

Blood is pumped to body

Bottom chamber contracts

MOST CAPILLARIES ARE SO NARROW THAT BLOOD CELLS PASS THROUGH ONE AT A TIME.

CLIMBERS SPEND ONLY MINUTES ON THE TOP OF MOUNT EVEREST AS THE THIN AIR IS DEADLY.

WHAT'S YOUR
BLOOD GROUP?

Everyone belongs to **one of four** main blood groups: **A, B, AB, and O.** The letters stand for molecules called *antigens* on the **surface of blood cells.** If you need blood from a donor, *choosing the right type is essential*—your immune system will **attack** antigens it doesn't recognize as your own.

Type A: You can receive only type A or O from a donor.

Type AB: You can receive blood from any donor.

Type O blood has no antigens.

Type B: You can receive only B or O from a donor.

Type O: You can receive only type O from a donor.

HOW SPEECH
WORKS

Your **voice** comes from your *vocal cords*—two flaps of tissue in your throat that **vibrate** when they're closed and air is forced between them. The *shape* of your mouth, lips, and tongue **change the sound** *to create speech.*

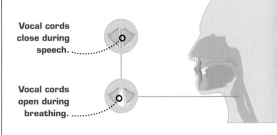

Vocal cords close during speech.

Vocal cords open during breathing.

TAKE A
DEEP BREATH

When you're *resting,* you breathe as few as **12 times a minute,** taking in up to **1 pint (0.5 liters)** of air each time. However, when you're *physically active,* both your breathing rate and the volume of each breath **increase** *so that more oxygen gets into your bloodstream.*

Resting
12 breaths a minute

Walking
20 breaths a minute

Jogging
40 breaths a minute

Running
70 breaths a minute

HIGHS AND LOWS

The longer and thicker your vocal cords are, *the deeper your voice.* The **pitch** of sounds is measured in units called *hertz (Hz),* which stand for **vibrations per second.**

← Lower pitch   Higher pitch →

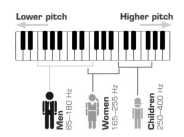

Men 85–180 Hz

Women 165–255 Hz

Children 250–400 Hz

STRANGE SOUNDS

Most of the time, you don't notice your chest **rising and falling** as you quietly *breathe.* Occasionally, however, your breathing system produces **strange or sudden** noises, such as laughs, snores, and yawns.

Laughter happens when your *vocal cords open and close repeatedly,* chopping sounds into **"ha ha ha"** segments.

Snoring happens when a *soft flap of tissue* at the back of your mouth *wobbles* as air passes over it.

Yawning draws a huge breath of air into the lungs while also *stretching muscles* around the throat.

SOME LIZARDS HAVE BRIGHT GREEN BLOOD.

AN ADAM'S APPLE IS A BUMP IN A MAN'S THROAT CAUSED BY HIS VOICE BOX.

Fueling the Body

Food supplies all the energy your body needs to keep working as well as raw materials for growth and repair. Before your body can use the valuable nutrients in food, you have to digest it.

Fresh fruits and vegetables are much better for your body than processed foods. The edible seeds of pomegranates contain at least 18 different vitamins and minerals and are a rich source of dietary fiber.

HOW IT WORKS

To stay healthy, you need a balanced diet. This should include a mix of the main food groups (carbohydrates, proteins, and fats) as well as at least five portions of fruits and vegetables a day.

Carbohydrates in foods such as potatoes and bread provide your body with energy.

Fiber keeps your digestive system healthy and is found in fruits and vegetables.

Proteins are needed for growth and repair and are found in foods such as beans and meat.

Fats are an essential part of all cells and also provide a long-term store of energy.

Different foods supply different amounts of energy. Food energy is measured in Calories (Cal) or kilojoules (kJ), which are shown on food labels. Adults need at least 2,000 Cal (8,400 kJ) a day.

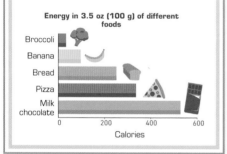

Energy in 3.5 oz (100 g) of different foods

Broccoli
Banana
Bread
Pizza
Milk chocolate

0   200   400   600
Calories

HOW MUCH
FOOD DO
YOU EAT?

Each day the average person chomps and slurps their way through 2–7 lb (1–3 kg) of food and drinks. Food is essential to keep your body healthy and working. Just as a phone needs regular charging, your body needs a regular supply of energy to keep you fit and active. Food also provides the raw materials your cells need for growth and repair. Eat too much food, however, and it can cause health problems that shorten your life span.

Food consumption varies a great deal from person to person and country to country. In wealthy parts of the world, some people consume too much, leading to health problems. In other places, people may get insufficient food or not enough variety in their diet, causing other health problems.

FAST FACTS

Every 60 seconds, the world consumes more than 5,000 tons of food.

Not all of the food the world produces is eaten—about one-third of it goes to waste.

 IN THE FUTURE, ASTRONAUTS MAY **RECYCLE POO** **TO MAKE FOOD.**

75%

5 ANIMAL AND 12 PLANT SPECIES SUPPLY 75% OF THE **WORLD'S FOOD.**

You'll consume about **55 tons** of food in your life, which is about the weight of **35 hippos.**

50%: RICE IS THE **MAIN FOOD** FOR 50% OF THE WORLD'S PEOPLE.

MORE THAN **2 BILLION** PEOPLE REGULARLY **EAT INSECTS.**

HOW MANY TEETH DO YOU HAVE?

How many teeth can you count with a finger? You may find only 20 or so, but you have a lot more hidden in your skull. Teeth are an essential part of your digestive system—they cut and mash food, making it easier for your body to break down and absorb. They can also trap bits of food between them, becoming a breeding ground for the bacteria that cause tooth decay if you forget to brush.

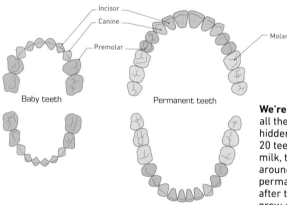

Incisor
Canine
Premolar
Molar
Baby teeth
Permanent teeth

We're born with buds of all the teeth we'll ever have hidden in our bones. The first 20 teeth to emerge are baby, or milk, teeth. They start falling out around the age of six, when permanent teeth appear. Look after these well because you won't grow a third set!

FAST FACTS

In total, you'll spend 80 days of your life brushing your teeth. Brushing removes plaque—a sticky layer of dirt and germs that builds up on teeth and causes decay.

Sharks don't need to brush their teeth since they keep growing new ones—up to 30,000 in one lifetime.

TOOTH DECAY IS DUE TO ACID FROM BACTERIA DISSOLVING THE MINERALS IN ENAMEL.

CATS CUT FLESH WITH TEETH THAT SLIDE PAST EACH OTHER LIKE SCISSORS.

HOW IT WORKS

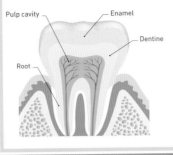

Pulp cavity
Enamel
Dentine
Root

The visible part of a tooth is the crown, which is made of enamel—a crystalline material that is the hardest substance in the human body. Under this is a bonelike substance called dentine, and inside that is a pulp cavity, a soft, sensitive tissue containing blood vessels and nerve cells.

Your permanent teeth are hidden in your skull until your baby teeth start falling out.

The roots of teeth are embedded in the skull.

By the age of six, humans have **52 teeth,** but most are **hidden in the skull.**

ELEPHANT TUSKS ARE HUGE INCISORS MADE MAINLY OF DENTINE.

THE IDEAL TIME TO BRUSH YOUR TEETH FOR IS 2 MINUTES.

What in the world?

INSIDE YOUR TEETH

Underneath the brittle outer shell of enamel that protects your teeth is a substance called dentine, seen here magnified 6,000 times by an electron microscope. Dentine has a honeycomb structure that makes it strong but allows sugary or sharp-tasting liquids from food to seep through if the enamel has a hole. These substances trigger nerve cells in the tooth's center, causing the pain of toothache.

HOW MUCH
SALIVA DO
YOU MAKE?

Here's a mouthwatering fact: every day you produce about 1 quart (1 liter) of saliva. Also known as spit, saliva helps you eat and digest food. As you chew, saliva mixes into the mashed-up food, making it soft and slimy so it's easier to swallow. Digestive chemicals in saliva also begin to break down the molecules in food.

HOW IT WORKS

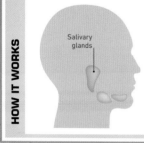

Salivary glands

Saliva is a mixture of water, salts, and various other substances, including a digestive enzyme—a chemical that helps break down food. It's pumped into your mouth by your salivary glands. You have three large salivary glands on each side of your face and about 1,000 tiny ones in your mouth, tongue, and throat.

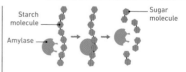

Starch molecule

Amylase

Sugar molecule

Saliva contains an enzyme called amylase, which breaks down starch molecules in foods like bread to form sugar molecules, which supply energy.

SALIVA IS 99% WATER.

SALIVA HELPS STOP ACIDIC FOODS FROM DAMAGING YOUR TEETH.

You'll produce enough saliva in your life to fill a bath about 150 times over. Your mouth makes saliva all the time and most of it gets swallowed, usually without you noticing. You swallow saliva about once a minute when not eating and about three times an hour when asleep.

Your mouth produces about 385 quarts (365 liters) of saliva a year.

FAST FACTS

Rats lick each other's wounds. Their saliva has a chemical in it that makes wounds heal twice as fast.

Cave-nesting birds in Southeast Asia use their sticky saliva to build nests on the walls of caves. The tiny nests have room for only two eggs each.

Venomous snakes use their fangs to inject saliva laced with deadly poisons into their prey. This lethal saliva is called venom.

Venom gland

A SNEEZE CAN SPRAY OUT MORE THAN 40,000 SALIVA DROPLETS.

YOU PRODUCE JUST 1 TEASPOONFUL OF SALIVA AN HOUR WHEN YOU SLEEP.

HOW BIG IS YOUR
STOMACH?

When you eat, your stomach expands. The space inside an empty stomach is about the volume of a plum, but a full stomach can expand to hold 50 times as much—about the volume of a soccer ball. Your stomach isn't just a storage space for food. It has powerful muscles that squeeze and grind food to mash it into a liquid, and glands in its wall produce digestive juices to break down the molecules in food.

The human stomach can expand to hold **75 hot dogs.**

With training, some people have increased their stomach capacity. American competitive eater Joey Chestnut consumed a record 75 hot dogs at an eating competition in 2020. He has also set records by eating 50 doughnuts, 52 cheeseburgers, 25.5 ice-cream sandwiches, 241 chicken wings, and 141 hard-boiled eggs!

FAST FACTS

Your stomach secretes a powerful chemical called hydrochloric acid, which can dissolve metal. This acid kills germs lurking in food and helps the stomach's digestive juices work.

A meal spends about four hours in the stomach.

The platypus has no stomach! Swallowed food goes straight into its intestines.

WHEN YOU **BLUSH,** THE LINING OF YOUR STOMACH **TURNS RED, TOO.**

YOUR STOMACH MAKES **3 QUARTS** (3 LITERS) OF DIGESTIVE JUICES EVERY DAY.

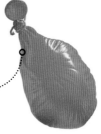

The space inside an empty stomach is about the same size as a plum.

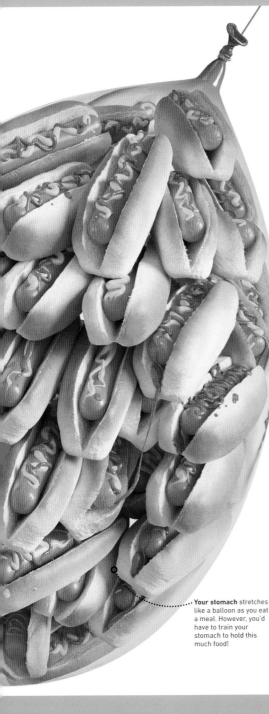

Your stomach stretches like a balloon as you eat a meal. However, you'd have to train your stomach to hold this much food!

HOW IT WORKS

The stomach's muscular wall has deep folds that help it stretch as it fills with food. Three different layers of muscle in the stomach wall can contract and relax in different patterns, squeezing food and mixing it up with liquid. After a few hours in the stomach, food turns into a soupy liquid called chyme.

As you eat a meal, the stomach fills with swallowed food and secretes gastric juice to digest it.

Muscles in the stomach wall contract in waves about three times a minute, squeezing and grinding the food.

When the food has turned into a liquid, a wave of contraction squirts it out through an opening called the pyloric sphincter.

A NEWBORN BABY'S STOMACH CAN HOLD ONLY ABOUT 2 TABLESPOONS OF FOOD.

TRIPE IS A FOOD MADE FROM THE STOMACHS OF COWS AND SHEEP.

What in the world?

GASTRIC PITS

In every square millimeter of the stomach's inner wall are 60–100 tiny pits, a few of which are seen here magnified 1,000 times in size by a microscope. At the base of these pits are glands that secrete a powerful acid and digestive enzymes to break down protein and fat in food. The stomach's digestive juices are so strong that the organ would digest itself if it didn't have special protection: a layer of thick, slimy mucus produced continually by its inner lining.

WHERE DOES
FOOD GO?

From the moment food enters your mouth, it embarks on an amazing adventure through your body. This journey full of twists and turns visits all the major organs of your 30 ft (9 m) long digestive system. As food passes through this maze of tubes and chambers, it breaks down into simple nutrients your bloodstream can absorb and carry away. The leftovers turn into a toxic waste that exits your body.

3:00 PM Absorbing nutrients
The inner lining of your small intestine is covered in millions of tiny, fingerlike projections called villi, which together create a huge surface area for absorbing digested food. Carbohydrates, proteins, and fats are broken down into simple molecules that pass into the villi and enter your blood.

IN

8:00 AM Into the mouth
When breakfast enters your mouth, your digestive system reacts immediately. As your teeth get chewing to break down the food, your mouth produces saliva—a digestive juice containing chemicals called enzymes, which break down food molecules.

8:01 AM Swallowing
Gulp! When you swallow, food doesn't just drop into your stomach; it gets there via a muscular tube called the esophagus, which pushes food along like toothpaste squeezed through a tube. Swallowing takes about 10 seconds.

8:01 AM
In the stomach
Depending on the size of a meal, food may spend about four hours in your stomach. This stretchy bag produces acid to kill germs and a digestive enzyme to break down protein. The muscular wall of your stomach churns food about until it turns into a thick, soupy liquid called chyme.

12:00 PM
Into the small intestine
Its job done, your stomach squirts the liquid food into your small intestine. Here, lots of different digestive enzymes are added to break down all the remaining nutrients in food.

THE AVERAGE PERSON SPENDS 4.5 YEARS OF THEIR LIFE EATING.

BACTERIA MAKE UP ABOUT HALF THE WEIGHT OF POO.

It takes **24–48 hours** for food to be digested and turned into **poo.**

5:00 PM Large intestine
After five or so hours in your small intestine, the watery, undigested remains of your breakfast reach the large intestine. Food spends at least 12 hours here as water is absorbed and billions of microscopic organisms called bacteria feed on the leftovers, transforming it into poo.

6:00 AM Feces form
As water is removed from the soup of bacteria and undigested matter, the mixture hardens to form a dense paste that breaks into lumps—feces. Fresh feces are stored in a chamber called the rectum until they are ready to be squeezed out by the rectum's muscular wall.

HOW IT WORKS

The digestive tract is a long tube that runs from your mouth to your anus. Along the way, organs such as the liver and pancreas add digestive juices containing enzymes. These attack the long chain molecules that make up proteins, carbohydrates, and fats, turning them into small molecules such as sugars and amino acids.

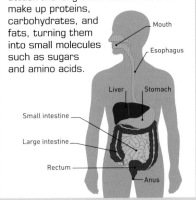

Mouth
Esophagus
Liver
Stomach
Small intestine
Large intestine
Rectum
Anus

8:00 AM
Final departure
Plop! Poo is pushed out of the anus and into the toilet. Don't forget to wash your hands!

OUT

THE STOMACH ACID OF CATS IS STRONG ENOUGH TO DISSOLVE BONE.

RABBITS EAT THEIR OWN POO TO GET ALL THE NUTRIENTS OUT OF FOOD.

What in the world?

INTESTINAL VILLI

Your small intestine doesn't just digest food—it also absorbs it. To do this effectively, it needs a very large surface area, so its inner surface is lined with small, fingerlike projections called villi. Each about 0.04 in (1 mm) long, these are just visible to the naked eye and give the inside of the small intestine a velvety texture. Each villus is packed with blood vessels to absorb and carry away the small, energy-rich molecules released when food is digested.

HOW MUCH PEE
DO YOU PEE?

Every day your body produces around 1.5 quarts (1.4 liters) of pee—more properly called urine. Urine is a waste liquid made by your kidneys, which filter the blood flowing around your body. They remove water that your body doesn't need as well as waste chemicals that would become deadly if they built up.

Your kidneys make about 130 gallons (500 liters) of urine a year (enough to fill two bathtubs) and about 10,500 gallons (40,000 liters) in your life, which is enough to fill a small swimming pool.

Pee gets its yellow color from the chemical urochrome, which is produced when old blood cells are broken down.

FAST FACTS

The human race has peed about 340 cubic miles (1,400 cubic kilometers) of urine so far. That's enough to keep Niagara Falls flowing for 19 years.

An empty bladder is about the size of a plum. When half full, it's about the size of an orange, while a full bladder reaches about the size of a grapefruit.

ASPARAGUS CONTAINS A CHEMICAL THAT CAN MAKE YOUR PEE SMELLY.

BIRDS EXCRETE A **WHITE** PASTE INSTEAD OF LIQUID URINE.

HOW IT WORKS

Urine is stored in an organ called the bladder, which stretches like a balloon as it fills up. Stretch receptors in the bladder's muscular wall tell your brain when you need to pee. To empty your bladder, you need to open two ring-shaped muscles called sphincters. The top one opens automatically, but the bottom one is voluntary, allowing you to control the flow.

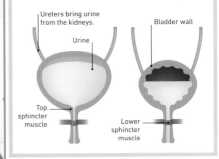

Ureters bring urine from the kidneys.

Urine

Top sphincter muscle

Bladder wall

Lower sphincter muscle

A lifetime of pee is enough to fill a **23 ft (7 m) long** swimming pool.

URINE IS RICH IN **NITROGEN** COMPOUNDS THAT HELP PLANTS GROW.

STALE ANIMAL URINE WAS ONCE USED TO MAKE **EXPLOSIVES.**

WHAT'S
YOUR PEE
MADE OF?

It might not look exciting, but your pee (urine) is a complex concoction of thousands of different chemicals, many of them harmful. It's made by your kidneys—two fist-sized organs on either side of your spine, just below your ribs. These organs work nonstop to filter unwanted or poisonous chemicals from your blood. The kidneys are essential to life. If they stopped working, you'd die in a matter of days.

INGREDIENTS:

FAST FACTS

Most large mammals take about the same time to pee: 21 seconds.

21 SEC

There's no truth in the claim that peeing on a jellyfish sting makes it feel better.

Scientists have identified more than 3,000 different waste compounds in urine.

The main ingredients in urine are water and urea, which is a nitrogen-rich compound produced when protein from food is broken down. There are also more than 3,000 other waste substances with mind-boggling chemical names. They come from many sources, including chemical reactions in your body cells, food, medicines, and bacteria living inside your body.

YOUR KIDNEYS FILTER ABOUT 48 GALLONS (180 LITERS) OF BLOOD EVERY DAY.

AN ELEPHANT'S BLADDER CAN HOLD 5 GALLONS (18 LITERS) OF PEE.

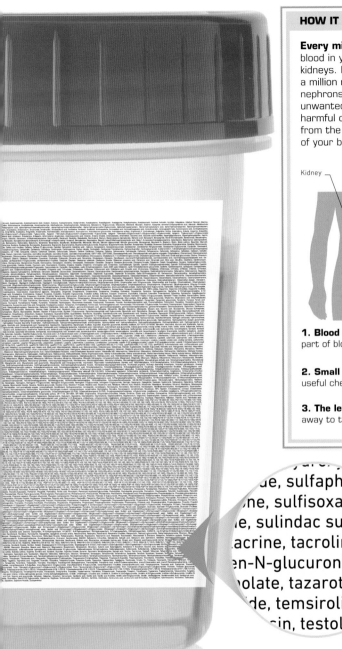

HOW IT WORKS

Every minute, about a quarter of the blood in your body passes through your kidneys. Each kidney contains more than a million microscopic filtering units called nephrons. These remove unwanted water and harmful chemicals from the liquid part of your blood.

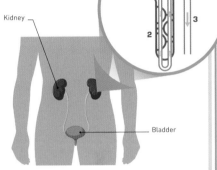

Kidney

Bladder

1. Blood enters a filtering unit and the liquid part of blood oozes out into a separate duct.

2. Small blood vessels reabsorb water and useful chemicals from the liquid in the duct.

3. The leftover water and chemicals drain away to the bladder as urine.

...e, sulfaphena...
...ne, sulfisoxazole, ...
...e, sulindac sulfone, s...
...acrine, tacrolimus, ta...
...en-N-glucuronide, tam...
...olate, tazarotene, ta...
...de, temsirolimus
...in, testola...

EVERY YEAR, MORE THAN 20,000 KIDNEY TRANSPLANTS TAKE PLACE IN THE US.

KIDNEY BEANS ARE SO NAMED BECAUSE THEY HAVE THE SAME SHAPE AS KIDNEYS.

HOW MUCH
WATER IS IN YOUR BODY?

More than half of your body is water. Water is essential to life because cells need it for all the chemical reactions that keep them alive. Having the right amount of water in your body is important so your brain continually monitors the water level in your blood and adjusts it as needed.

The amount of water in your body depends mainly on your age. A newborn baby is about three-quarters water because water-rich organs like the lungs, brain, and muscles make up most of its body. As people get older, their water level falls because muscles get thinner.

Young adult: 57% water

FAST FACTS

Kangaroo rats live in deserts and never drink water. Their cells make water from food molecules by a chemical reaction.

90%

About 90 percent of the water in your body comes from food and drink. The rest is made by your body cells.

A camel can drink 26 gallons (100 liters) of water in 10 minutes after a desert trek.

YOU CAN LOSE MORE THAN **HALF A PINT** (0.25 LITERS) OF WATER A DAY IN YOUR BREATH.

YOUR BONES ARE **31%** WATER.

HOW IT WORKS

If the water level in your body drops, your brain triggers a feeling of thirst. It also releases a hormone that travels to your kidneys and tells them to reabsorb water from urine (which makes your urine darker). When your body's water level is high, you stop feeling thirsty and your kidneys let more water escape into urine (which makes your urine pale).

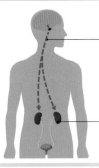

Your brain sends a hormone to your kidneys, telling them how much water to remove from your blood.

Your kidneys adjust how much water goes into urine.

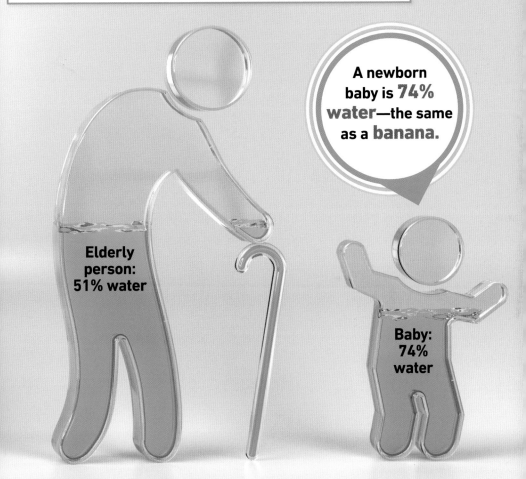

A newborn baby is **74% water**—the same as a **banana.**

Elderly person: 51% water

Baby: 74% water

YOUR BRAIN AND HEART ARE 73% WATER.

YOU CAN SURVIVE FOR ONLY ABOUT THREE DAYS WITHOUT WATER.

Food and Digestion Facts

ENERGY *NEEDS*

Food provides **energy** to *fuel your body cells* and keep you alive. The amount of energy you need depends on your **age**, **sex**, and **how active you are**.

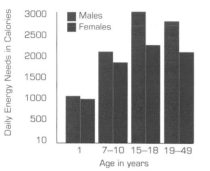

Daily Energy Needs in Calories — Age in years: 1, 7–10, 15–18, 19–49
Legend: Males, Females

ENERGY IN FOOD

Foods vary a lot in **energy content**. You get energy from **fats**, **carbohydrates**, and **proteins**, but fats have about *twice as much energy* as carbohydrates and proteins. Your body uses energy all the time, but you use more when you're **physically active**. This chart shows how quickly you would use up the energy in different foods by running.

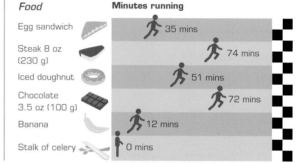

Food	Minutes running
Egg sandwich	35 mins
Steak 8 oz (230 g)	74 mins
Iced doughnut	51 mins
Chocolate 3.5 oz (100 g)	72 mins
Banana	12 mins
Stalk of celery	0 mins

ENERGY AND EXERCISE

Your body uses energy all the time, even when you're resting. The **harder your body works**, the **more energy you use**. A banana contains about **100 calories** of energy, which sustains *different types of* **activities** for *different lengths of* **time**.

Fast swimming 10 minutes | Casual cycling 20 minutes | Walking 25 minutes | Sleeping 2 hours

FOOD FROM GRASS

Everyone knows that **sheep and cows** are **mainly grass eaters**, but did you know that **humans** are **mainly grass eaters, too**? About *two-thirds of the food calories we eat* come from **cultivated grasses called cereals**, such as wheat, rice, and corn.

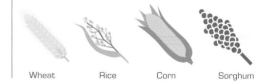

Wheat | Rice | Corn | Sorghum

AN **AFRICAN LUNGFISH** CAN SURVIVE FOR **4 YEARS** WITHOUT A MEAL.

WOMBATS ARE THE ONLY ANIMALS THAT DO **CUBE-SHAPED POOS**.

DIGESTIVE *SYSTEMS*

The length of an animal's digestive system depends on its **body size** and the **kind of food** it eats. **Plant material** is harder to digest than **meat**, so *plant-eating animals* have the **longest digestive systems**.

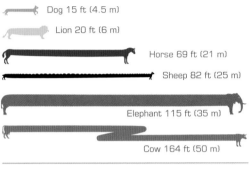

Dog 15 ft (4.5 m)

Lion 20 ft (6 m)

Horse 69 ft (21 m)

Sheep 82 ft (25 m)

Elephant 115 ft (35 m)

Cow 164 ft (50 m)

WASTE DISPOSAL

Waste from your **digestive system** leaves your body as **poo**, but poo isn't just undigested food. It's **mainly water** and **microorganisms called bacteria**. Most of the bacteria are harmless and *help your body process food*, but some can **spread disease**—so always remember to *wash your hands*.

Contents of poo

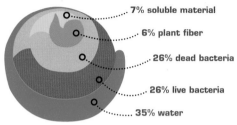

- 7% soluble material
- 6% plant fiber
- 26% dead bacteria
- 26% live bacteria
- 35% water

WATER IN *WATER OUT*

Every cell in your body needs water. Water also makes **blood** flow, controls **temperature**, lubricates **joints**, and moistens your **eyes**, **mouth**, **airways**, and **digestive system**. You gain and lose water in several ways, but your **brain** and **kidneys** ensure your body's water level *stays balanced*.

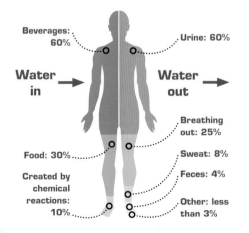

Beverages: 60%

Water in →

Food: 30%

Created by chemical reactions: 10%

Urine: 60%

Water out →

Breathing out: 25%

Sweat: 8%

Feces: 4%

Other: less than 3%

CURIOUS CUISINES

Some foods, such as *burgers and fries*, are **extremely popular**. Others, however, have **flavors** that most people find **hard to stomach**.

Fermented herring is salted and *then left raw* for several months to develop an overpowering **stench**.

The **durian fruit** has a delicious *sweet taste* but an *odor* likened to **rotten onions**, **vomit**, or **sewage**.

Casu marzu is a sheep's cheese containing hundreds of *live maggots*.

Civet coffee is made from **coffee beans** that have been *eaten and pooed out* by animals called **civets**.

Century eggs are *preserved in clay* until they *turn green* and develop an intense **rotten smell**.

Rocky Mountain oysters are not real oysters at all—they are deep fried **bulls' testicles**.

ADULT MAYFLIES NEVER POO.

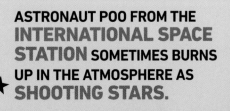

ASTRONAUT POO FROM THE INTERNATIONAL SPACE STATION SOMETIMES BURNS UP IN THE ATMOSPHERE AS **SHOOTING STARS.**

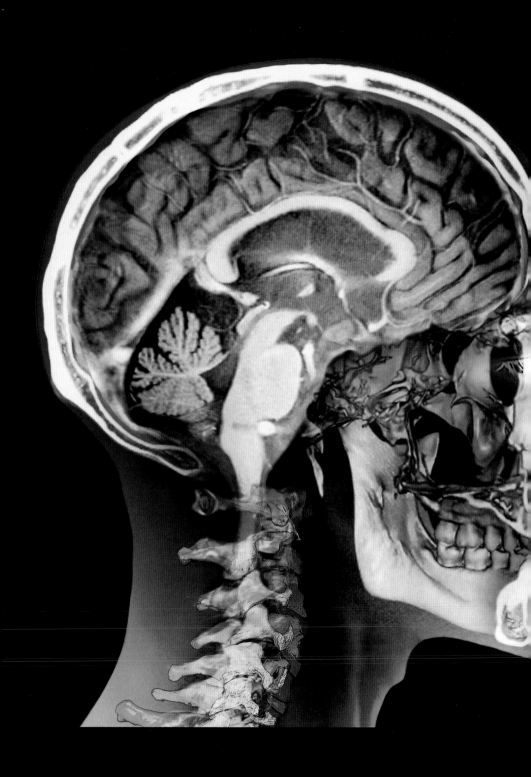

Control

Every second, trillions of electrical signals zoom through the vast web of interconnected cells that makes up your brain. The control center of the nervous system, the brain is the most complex and mysterious organ in the human body.

The human brain is mostly fat, which makes it difficult to see on X-rays. This composite image combines 3-D X-ray images of a man's head with a magnetic resonance imaging (MRI) scan. The MRI scan makes his brain's soft tissues visible.

Neurons, or nerve cells, look very different from the other cells in your body. They have long, spindly fibers that carry electrical signals to and from other cells. Incoming signals travel along fibers called dendrites. Outgoing signals travel along longer, faster fibers called axons.

Junctions between neurons are called synapses.

The central part of a neuron is called the cell body.

HOW FAST
IS A NERVE
SIGNAL?

Your body is controlled by a high-speed data network called your nervous system. It's made up of billions of wirelike cells called neurons, which conduct electrical signals around your body at speeds of up to 179 mph (288 km/h). Neurons carry signals from your sense organs to your brain—your body's central computer—to make you aware of the world. They also carry outgoing signals to your muscles and other organs, telling your body how to react.

YOUR **LONGEST NERVE** RUNS FROM YOUR BIG TOE TO YOUR SPINE.

BRAINS SHRINK BY ABOUT 5% PER DECADE AFTER THE AGE OF 40.

HOW IT WORKS

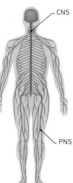

Most of your neurons are in your brain and spine, which make up your central nervous system (CNS). The central nervous system is connected to the rest of your body by bundles of neurons called nerves. These nerves make up your peripheral nervous system (PNS).

CNS

PNS

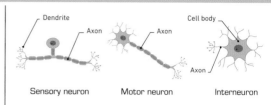

Dendrite

Axon

Axon

Cell body

Axon

Sensory neuron

Motor neuron

Interneuron

Different types of neurons do different jobs. Sensory neurons carry signals from your sense organs to your brain. Motor neurons carry signals from your brain to your muscles. Your brain consists mostly of interneurons, which form complex circuits to store information.

All neurons have long, wirelike projections that carry electrical signals.

Electrical signals shoot through your brain at the speed of a **Formula One racing car.**

FAST FACTS

The fastest-known nerve signals belong to a type of shrimp and travel at about 470 mph (760 km/h).

There are around 86 billion neurons in the human brain.

20%

20% OF THE ENERGY IN YOUR FOOD IS USED BY YOUR BRAIN.

FAST FACTS

Your brain can be just as active during a dream as when you're awake.

Starfish, sea urchins, jellyfish, and other headless animals have no brains.

Your brain has billions of neurons (nerve cells), each of which may have thousands of connections to other neurons. Information is stored in this huge web of connections. It's difficult to calculate exactly how much information the human brain stores as it doesn't work quite like a computer. Some scientists estimate it can hold about 1 petabyte (1 million gigabytes) of data, but others think it could be even more.

THE AVERAGE **BRAIN** WEIGHS 2.9 LB (1.3 KG).

2.9 lb (1.3 kg)

SHORT-TERM MEMORIES LAST FOR AS LITTLE AS **15 SECONDS.**

HOW MUCH
INFORMATION CAN YOUR BRAIN STORE?

Your brain can store enough information to fill a shelf of books **9 times wider** than planet Earth.

Your brain is incredible. This mass of cells about the size of a head of cauliflower creates your inner world of thoughts, feelings, memories, dreams, and experiences. How it does all of this is still largely a mystery. However, scientists think the brain's ability to store and process information comes from the way its cells connect in circuits called neural networks.

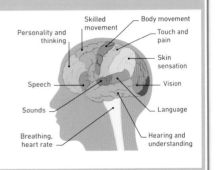

Your brain can store at least one petabyte of data, which is enough to fill 5 billion books of 0.2 megabytes each.

HOW IT WORKS

Your brain is made up of distinct areas that carry out different tasks. For example, the area in charge of vision is at the back of your brain, while a strip above your ear helps you move. However, many processes involve networks of neurons spread across the brain. Memories, for instance, are stored as patterns of connections between many parts of your brain.

Personality and thinking
Skilled movement
Body movement
Touch and pain
Skin sensation
Speech
Vision
Sounds
Language
Breathing, heart rate
Hearing and understanding

THE **RIGHT** SIDE OF YOUR BRAIN CONTROLS THE **LEFT** SIDE OF YOUR BODY AND VICE VERSA.

A NEWBORN BABY'S BRAIN IS ABOUT **10%** OF ITS BODY WEIGHT.

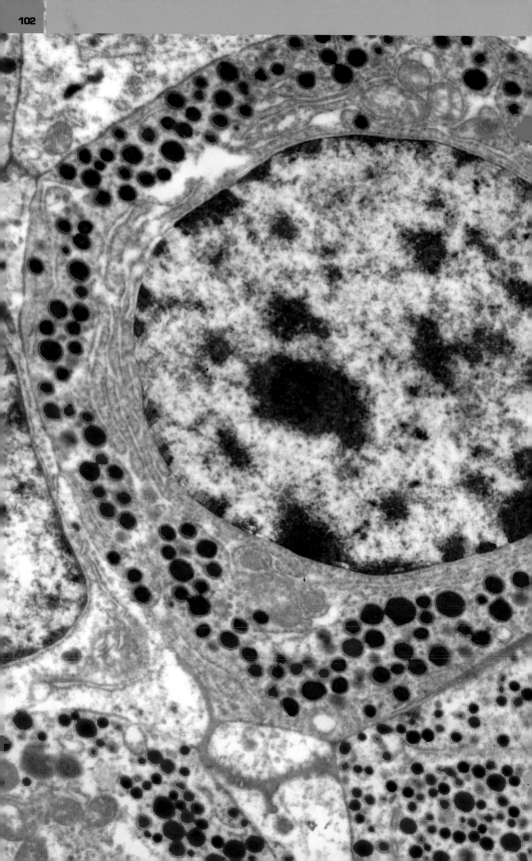

What in the world?

GROWTH HORMONE

The large green cell in this microscope image produces the hormone that makes humans grow. While you're fast asleep, cells like this in the base of your brain release growth hormone, which makes your bones longer, your muscles thicker, and every major organ except your brain larger. The cells are called somatotrophs and store the hormone in tiny granules, which appear brown in this image. Sleep well if you want to be tall—your growth hormone level peaks during deep sleep.

Brain and Nerve Facts

GET CONNECTED

Your brain learns and remembers by forming *connections* between neurons to create **neural networks**. The number of neural networks your brain can create is **infinite**.

REFLEX ACTIONS

Sometimes you **need to react** before you have *time to think*. Your quickest reactions are **reflexes** and happen without any input from your brain. The nerve signal in a reflex travels from a **sensory cell** to your spinal cord and then **straight to the muscles** that make you react.

The knee-jerk reflex straightens your leg when the soft tissue in your knee joint stretches, which helps you stand.

Your pupils dilate (widen) and constrict (shrink) automatically to help you see when it gets darker or brighter.

A reflex blink closes your eye if anything touches your eye or an eyelash.

The gag reflex makes your throat contract, protecting you from choking on something too big to swallow safely.

Vomiting is a reflex triggered by your stomach if you swallow something harmful.

MIND THE GAP

The connections between neurons are called **synapses**. Electrical signals *can't cross* these as they contain tiny gaps. Instead, chemicals called neurotransmitters are released. They cross the gap and **stimulate the cell** on the other side.

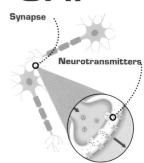

Synapse

Neurotransmitters

BRAINWAVES

Scientists can monitor a person's **brain activity** by placing sensors on their scalp to pick up faint electrical signals from neurons. This technique creates patterns called **brain waves**, which reveal whether the brain is active, resting, or asleep. **Abnormal patterns** are a sign of disease.

Human brain waves

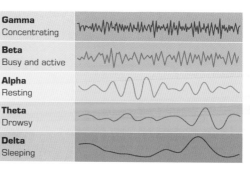

Gamma Concentrating	
Beta Busy and active	
Alpha Resting	
Theta Drowsy	
Delta Sleeping	

THE HUMAN BRAIN RUNS ON 20 WATTS OF POWER.

AN ELEPHANT'S NERVOUS SYSTEM HAS 260 BILLION NEURONS.

HOW MUCH SLEEP?

You'll spend about **a third of your life** *asleep*. How much sleep you need each night depends on **your age**. As we get older, we need less sleep and tend to wake earlier.

Changes in your brain's *internal clock* **make waking in the morning hardest in your teenage years.**

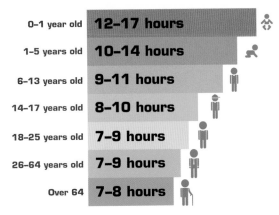

Age	Hours
0–1 year old	**12–17 hours**
1–5 years old	**10–14 hours**
6–13 years old	**9–11 hours**
14–17 years old	**8–10 hours**
18–25 years old	**7–9 hours**
26–64 years old	**7–9 hours**
Over 64	**7–8 hours**

SLEEP *CYCLES*

Regular sleep is essential for the **health of your brain**, though exactly why is largely a *mystery to science.* During a night's sleep, your brain cycles through five different **sleep stages** that have distinctive brain waves and different levels of activity. Dreaming occurs in rapid eye movement (REM) sleep, when your **eyes dart about** under your eyelids.

Awake
You're fully aware and alert.

Stage 1
You feel drowsy but half awake.

Stage 2
Body temperature and heart rate fall.

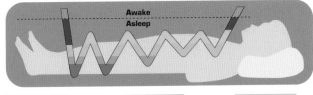

Stage 3
Brain waves slow as sleep deepens.

Stage 4
Very deep sleep. You are difficult to wake.

REM sleep
Eyes move rapidly and dreams occur.

WHAT'S *YOUR* EQ?

Who's smarter, a dolphin or a chimp? We can't tell *how intelligent animals are* from their **brain size** as larger animals have larger brains. So scientists sometimes use a measure called **EQ** (encephalization quotient), which takes account of body size. **Humans have an EQ of 7.5**, which means our brains are *7.5 times larger than expected for our size.*

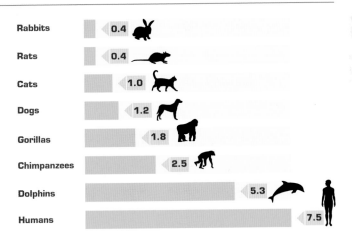

Animal	EQ
Rabbits	0.4
Rats	0.4
Cats	1.0
Dogs	1.2
Gorillas	1.8
Chimpanzees	2.5
Dolphins	5.3
Humans	7.5

A SNAIL'S NERVOUS SYSTEM HAS 11,000 NEURONS.

A SEA SPONGE HAS NO NEURONS AND NO BRAIN.

Super Senses

Vision, hearing, smell, taste, and touch are your main senses—but far from your only ones. Sense organs send a continual stream of data to your brain. Your brain uses this information to build a multicolor inner world of experience and sensation.

If a person loses their vision, other senses can sometimes compensate. Braille books use patterns of bumps to represent words, allowing people to read by touch instead of sight.

HOW MANY
SENSES DO
YOU HAVE?

You probably think you've got five senses: vision, hearing, smell, taste, and touch. Wrong! Humans have far more than five senses. Your body can also sense temperature, pain, gravity, movement, the positions of your limbs, the stretching of your muscles, and the fullness of internal organs, from your bladder to your stomach.

Your sense of balance lets you stand, walk, and run without falling over. The main organ of balance is inside your inner ear.

Sound waves travel invisibly through the air all the time. They are captured by your ears, which give you the sense of hearing.

Pain receptors are all over and inside your body. They help protect it from injuries.

HOW IT WORKS

All senses use sensory cells—nerve cells that send electrical signals to the brain when they sense certain "stimuli," such as light, sound, touch, chemicals, or heat. Your brain makes you aware and figures out how your body should react. If rapid action is needed, your brain sends signals to your muscles.

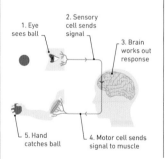

Your motion sensors are inside three hoops called semicircular canals.

An ear doesn't just sense sound—it also detects motion and gravity. Your inner ear has three tiny, fluid-filled hoops containing motion sensors that are triggered when the fluid sloshes about. This system can detect different kinds of head movement, such as rotating, tilting, and rising or falling.

1. Eye sees ball
2. Sensory cell sends signal
3. Brain works out response
5. Hand catches ball
4. Motor cell sends signal to muscle

Rotating   Tilting   Rising/falling

BALANCE IS A SENSE THAT YOU CAN LEARN TO IMPROVE.

SPINNING MAKES YOU DIZZY BECAUSE IT MOVES THE FLUID IN YOUR INNER EAR.

Your eyes capture and focus light to give you the sense of vision.

Motion sensors in your ears detect movements of your head.

Your nose can detect trillions of different odor molecules floating in the air.

Your tongue has thousands of taste buds that sense whether food is sweet, salty, bitter, sour, or savory.

Your skin has millions of receptors that sense different kinds of touch and pressure.

Sensory cells inside muscles and joints sense the position and movement of every part of your body.

Temperature receptors in your skin, mouth, eyes, and other places react to heat and cold. You feel extreme temperatures as pain.

When your stomach fills up, stretch receptors in its wall trigger a feeling of fullness.

When your bladder or rectum is full, stretch receptors in their walls trigger the sensation of needing to visit the toilet.

Your body has at least 12 senses.

FAST FACTS

Animals can sense things that humans can't.

Bees can see ultraviolet colors. This helps them spot patterns in flowers that have nectar.

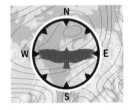

Birds sense Earth's magnetic field, giving them a built-in compass to find their way on long journeys.

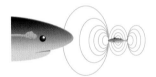

Sharks and other fish can sense the electric fields around prey.

Most mammals have whiskers, though we don't. Whiskers can touch things and feel air movements. They tell an animal whether a hole is big enough to squeeze its whole body through.

108°F (42°C) IS THE TEMPERATURE AT WHICH HEAT FEELS PAINFUL.

THERE ARE MORE THAN 3,000 TOUCH RECEPTORS IN A FINGERTIP.

HOW MANY
COLORS CAN YOU SEE?

Your eyes are windows onto the world. They take in light and focus it to make images, giving you the sense of vision. The colors you see are captured by special cells called cones in the back of your eyeballs. Humans have three kinds of cone cells, but by working together, they can detect millions of different colors. Some animals have more types of cones than we do and see colors invisible to us.

The colors of the rainbow make up what we call the spectrum. There are only seven main colors in spectrum (red, orange, yellow, green, blue, indigo, violet), but between these are many other shades. Every color in the spectrum comes from light waves with a particular wavelength. However, our brains also create imaginary colors that don't exist in the spectrum by blending real colors together. We see magenta, for instance, when blue and red light mix.

FAST FACTS

Cats and dogs have only two types of cone cells, so they see fewer colors than we see. Birds, reptiles, and amphibians have four types of cone cells and see colors we never see.

Eagles can see five times farther than humans, letting them spot prey while flying. With eyes like an eagle's, you could read your phone screen from across a room.

The eyes of tarsiers are larger than their brains. The tarsier has poor color vision but can see very well at night when it hunts insects. The largest eyes in the animal world belong to the colossal squid and are as big as basketballs.

THE PATTERN IN THE COLORED PART OF YOUR EYE IS UNIQUE, LIKE A FINGERPRINT.

INSECT COMPOUND EYES ARE MADE OF THOUSANDS OF TINY UNITS.

HOW IT WORKS

An eye is a jelly-filled ball with a single hole—a pupil—to let in light. Like a camera, an eye has a lens that focuses light onto a sensitive layer at the back, the retina. The retina is lined with millions of cone cells and rod cells. Cones detect colors, and rods work in dim light, so you can still see at night but with much less color.

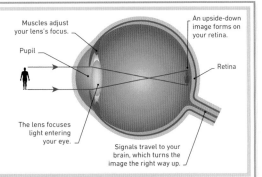

Muscles adjust your lens's focus.

Pupil

An upside-down image forms on your retina.

Retina

The lens focuses light entering your eye.

Signals travel to your brain, which turns the image the right way up.

The human eye might be able to see up to **10 million different colors.**

THE TUATARA LIZARD HAS A **THIRD EYE** IT USES TO KEEP TRACK OF TIME.

BLINKING CLEANS AND MOISTENS THE **SURFACE** OF YOUR EYES.

What in the world?

CONES AND RODS

Your sense of vision relies on two types of light-detecting cells in your eyes: cones and rods. Cones (colored green in this microscope image) can detect color, but they need bright light to work well. They are packed especially densely right in the center of your field of vision, providing high definition and rich color in whatever object you're looking at directly. Rods (blue in this image) can't sense color, but they are more sensitive. They give you night vision, which has almost no color and is slightly blurry.

How Do Illusions Work?

You can't always believe your eyes! Your sense of vision depends on your brain as much as your eyes, but your brain uses shortcuts to process the stream of data from your eyes and figure out what you're looking at. Optical illusions take advantage of these shortcuts to trick you into seeing things that aren't really there.

Phantom shapes
In this illusion, you see what looks like a white square or triangle, but the shapes aren't actually there. Your brain interprets the black shapes as circles, so it assumes there's a white shape in front that partly blocks the view.

Size comparison
The part of your brain that processes vision judges the size of objects by comparing them to what's next to them. Here, the surrounding black circles trick your brain into seeing the left red circle as larger than the right one, but they're exactly the same.

Vanishing colors
Hold the page close, stare at the center, and count to 30 without moving your eyes. The colors will vanish. If light-detecting cells in your eyes keep sending the same signal repeatedly to the brain, they tire and briefly stop working.

MOUNTAINS LOOK CLOSER ON CLEAR DAYS BECAUSE OUR BRAINS USE HAZE TO JUDGE DISTANCE.

BRAIN SCANS SHOW THAT ILLUSIONS ACTIVATE THE SAME PARTS OF A BRAIN AS REAL IMAGES.

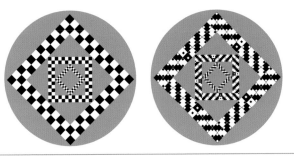

Wonky squares

All the sides in these squares are perfectly straight, but the squares on the right look wonky. The dots inside the small black and white squares trick your brain, but exactly how is a mystery. Take away the dots and the illusion stops.

Illusory color

There is no red in this image—the tomatoes are the same shade of gray as the band at the bottom. Your brain creates an illusory red color because the cyan tint tricks it into perceiving the opposite color in gray parts of the picture.

Illusory motion

Does this pattern seem to move when you move your eyes? Your brain uses sudden changes in contrast to sense motion. This picture uses a high-contrast pattern to fool that system and create illusory motion as your eyes move.

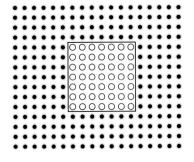

Floating circles

Do the white spots appear to float above the black spots? Your brain judges distance from what's in focus. Here, the white spots are sharp but the black spots are blurry, making them look farther away. The raft of white spots may also appear to jiggle if you move your eyes around the image.

ARTISTS USE ILLUSIONS TO CREATE DEPTH IN PICTURES.

COMPUTERS CAN BE PROGRAMMED TO BE FOOLED BY OPTICAL ILLUSIONS.

What in the world?

OTOLITH

When you tilt a phone, a tiny device inside it—an accelerometer—swings sideways and triggers a circuit that keeps the display upright. Your body uses just the same trick when you tilt or turn your head. Inside your inner ears are otoliths—tiny clusters of calcium carbonate crystals attached to sensory hairs. When you move your head, the weight of the otoliths makes them sway, triggering nerve signals to your brain. Your brain compares these signals to input from your eyes to keep your vision stable and your body balanced.

HOW MANY THINGS
CAN YOU TASTE?

Most of the flavor you get from food doesn't come from your mouth—it comes from your nose. The taste buds in your mouth sense only five distinct tastes, but your nose can distinguish about 1 trillion different odors. When you're eating, the tastes and smells of the food combine in your brain to give everything a unique flavor. On top of that, the texture, temperature, and crunching sound of foods affect the way you experience them.

FAST FACTS

The distinctive smells of things often come from the way many different odor molecules combine. The smell of bananas comes from up to 300 odor chemicals. Tomatoes produce about 400 odor chemicals, and coffee produces over 600.

The heat of chiles comes from pain receptors, not taste buds. Chile heat is measured in Scoville Heat Units (SHU), with jalapeños measuring about 5,000 SHUs. The hottest chile, the Carolina reaper, has 2.2 million SHU.

HOW IT WORKS

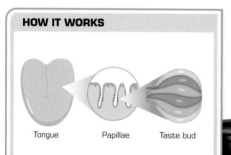

Tongue   Papillae   Taste bud

Your sense of taste comes from taste buds—tiny clusters of sensory cells in your mouth. Most are found in tiny bumps called papillae on your tongue. When you put food in your mouth, saliva dissolves taste chemicals and carries them to your taste buds, which send signals to your brain.

Olfactory bulb

Odors reach your nose before you even start eating. When you chew, odor molecules enter your nose from the back of your mouth. They land on your olfactory bulb, which then sends signals to your brain.

Bitterness is one of the five main tastes. Bitter food and drinks include orange peel, coffee, unripe fruit, and the leaves of many plants.

Sweet food has sugar in it. Different kinds of sugar include sucrose (table sugar) and fructose (the natural sugar in fruit).

SOME FISH HAVE
TASTE BUDS
ON THEIR BODY
SURFACE AND TAIL.

THE MEDICAL
CONDITION AGEUSIA
MEANS YOU HAVE **NO**
SENSE OF TASTE.

The surface of your tongue is covered with tiny bumps called papillae.

Your mouth can sense only five tastes: bitter, sweet, salty, sour, and umami.

Salty food contains mineral salts, such as sodium chloride (table salt). This is what we sprinkle on French fries.

Sour food and drinks contain acids, such as the citric acid in lemon juice or acetic acid in vinegar.

Umami is the Japanese word for savory. Foods that taste savory include cooked meat, gravy, and soy sauce.

THE AVERAGE LIFE SPAN OF A TASTE BUD IS 10 DAYS.

IF YOU'RE HUNGRY, CHANGES IN YOUR BRAIN MAKE FOOD TASTE BETTER.

WHAT'S THE
SMALLEST BONE
IN THE BODY?

The tiniest bone in the human body is called the stapes. It's no bigger than a sesame seed and lies hidden deep inside your ear. Together with two other tiny bones, the stapes forms a lever mechanism that amplifies sound waves captured by your eardrum, before transferring them to your inner ear, which creates your sense of hearing.

The stapes gets its name from the Latin word for stirrup, as the bone looks just like the foot stirrup used in horse riding. An ant would have no difficulty carrying this tiny bone—it weighs a mere 0.0001 oz (3 mg), which is about one-tenth of the weight of a grain of rice.

FAST FACTS

The speed of sound in air is one-millionth of the speed of light. This is why you see the flash of lightning several seconds before hearing the rumble of thunder.

Elephants can hear through the soles of their feet. Their deep, rumbling calls produce vibrations that travel for miles through the ground, letting the animals communicate over long distances.

THE VOLUME OF SOUND IS MEASURED IN DECIBELS.

THE WORD COCHLEA COMES FROM THE GREEK WORD FOR SNAIL SHELL.

At **0.1 in (3 mm)** long, the stapes bone is one-third the length of a carpenter ant.

Ants have no ears. They pick up sounds with their antennae.

HOW IT WORKS

Your ears collect sound waves—invisible ripples that speed through the air. Sounds are funneled to your eardrum, a vibrating circle of skin that moves the stapes and other ear bones as sound waves hit it. The tiny bones transfer the movements to your fluid-filled inner ear, where the sounds travel inside a snail-shaped tube called the cochlea. This pea-sized organ contains nerve cells that pick up the vibrations and send signals to your brain.

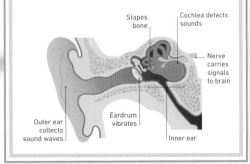

Stapes bone

Cochlea detects sounds

Nerve carries signals to brain

Outer ear collects sound waves

Eardrum vibrates

Inner ear

SALAMANDERS CAN **HEAR** THROUGH THEIR **LUNGS.**

EARWAX TASTES NASTY BECAUSE IT CONTAINS ACIDS THAT KILL GERMS.

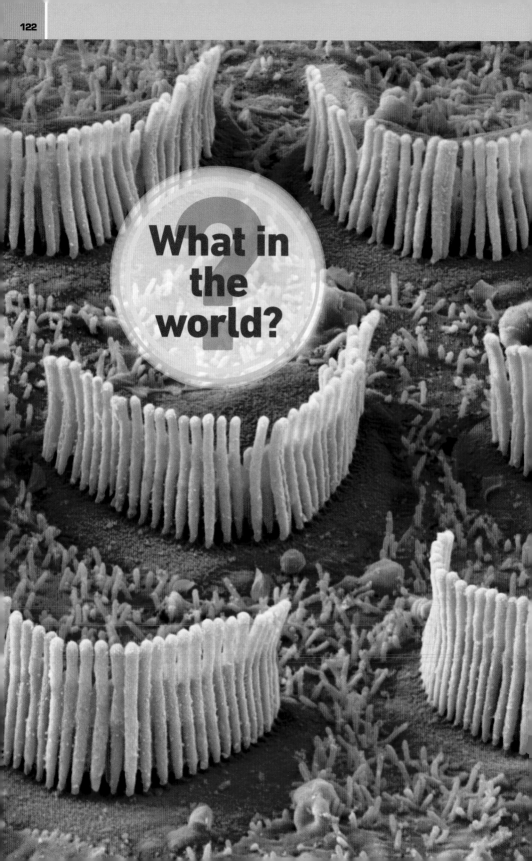

What in the world?

STEREOCILIA

These microscopic hairs are the tips of the sound-detecting cells that create the sense of hearing. Sound waves captured by the ears are funneled into the inner ear, where they travel through fluid like ripples. The ripples bend these tiny hairs back and forth, triggering nerve signals that travel to the brain. The hairs are called stereocilia and are seen here magnified 25,000 times in size by an electron microscope.

Senses Facts

HOW LOUD?

The **loudness (volume)** of sound depends on how much **energy** there is in the **sound waves**. Loudness is measured in units called **decibels (dB)**.

Jet taking off
110–140 dB

Lawnmower
about 90 dB

Laughter
about 60 dB

Leaves rustling
about 10 dB

220
200
180
160
140
120
100
80
60
40
20

Atomic bomb
210 dB (the loudest sound ever made by humans)

Thunder
about 120 dB

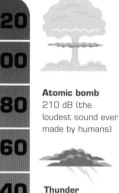

Washing machine
about 80 dB

Mosquito's whine
about 20 dB

Limit of human
hearing: 0 dB

HEARING *RANGE*

The **pitch**, or **frequency**, of a sound (*whether it is high or low*) is measured in **hertz (Hz)**. Humans hear sounds between **20 and 20,000 Hz**. Sound higher than this is called **ultrasound**, while **infrasound** is sound too low for us to hear. Some animals *can hear ultrasound or infrasound*.

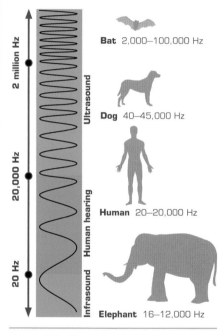

2 million Hz
20,000 Hz
20 Hz

Ultrasound
Human hearing
Infrasound

Bat 2,000–100,000 Hz

Dog 40–45,000 Hz

Human 20–20,000 Hz

Elephant 16–12,000 Hz

FAR *VIEW*

The **most distant object** you can see with the unaided eye is the **Andromeda Galaxy**, a mind-boggling **2.5 million** light-years away. That means you see it as it was 2.5 million years ago.

YOUR FINGERTIPS HAVE **100 TIMES** MORE TOUCH RECEPTORS PER SQUARE INCH THAN THE SKIN ON YOUR BACK.

FLIES CAN TASTE FOOD WITH **THEIR FEET.**

CONE COLORS

Our eyes have **three types** of color-detecting **cone cells**, which are sensitive to **red**, **green**, and **blue** light. Combined, they can detect **millions of colors**, all made of **mixtures** of these *three basic colors*.

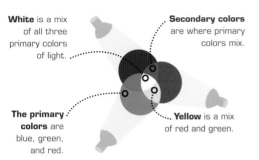

White is a mix of all three primary colors of light.

Secondary colors are where primary colors mix.

The primary colors are blue, green, and red.

Yellow is a mix of red and green.

COLOR BLINDNESS

Can you see the **number eight** here? In some people, one of the *three types of cone cells* is **defective**, causing **reduced color vision**. This is called **color blindness**, even though most *colors are still visible*.

Red-green color blindness test

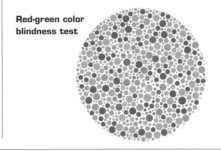

SUPER SNIFFERS

Using their amazing **long-distance sense of smell**, some animals can **sniff out** a mate, food, or danger *many miles away*.

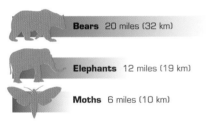

Bears 20 miles (32 km)

Elephants 12 miles (19 km)

Moths 6 miles (10 km)

READ BY TOUCH

Many **blind people** use their *sensitive fingertips* to read using the **Braille system**, in which patterns of **raised dots** *represent letters and numbers*.

HELLO

Letters are formed by patterns of up to six dots.

SEEING IN THE DARK

Animals with **good night vision** tend to have a higher ratio of **rods to cones** in their eyes. They have *poor color vision*, but they can see in a **fraction of the amount of light** that we need.

▲ Large eyes
An **owl's eyes** can account for **3 percent** of its body weight. Our own eyes make up *just 0.02 percent of our weight*.

▲ Wide pupils
The eyes of many nighttime animals have **pupils** that **open incredibly wide** to let in as much light as possible.

▲ Reflective layer
Cats' eyes have a **shiny layer** called a **tapetum**. It *bounces light around* inside the eye so that **more light is detected**.

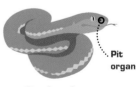

Pit organ

▲ Seeing heat
Some snakes use special **pit organs** on their head to "see" **infrared (heat) waves** given off by *warm-blooded prey* at night.

SEALS USE THEIR WHISKERS TO **DETECT FISH** UP TO **330 FT (100 M)** AWAY.

YOU HAVE SPECIAL TOUCH **RECEPTORS** TO DETECT **TICKLES AND ITCHES.**

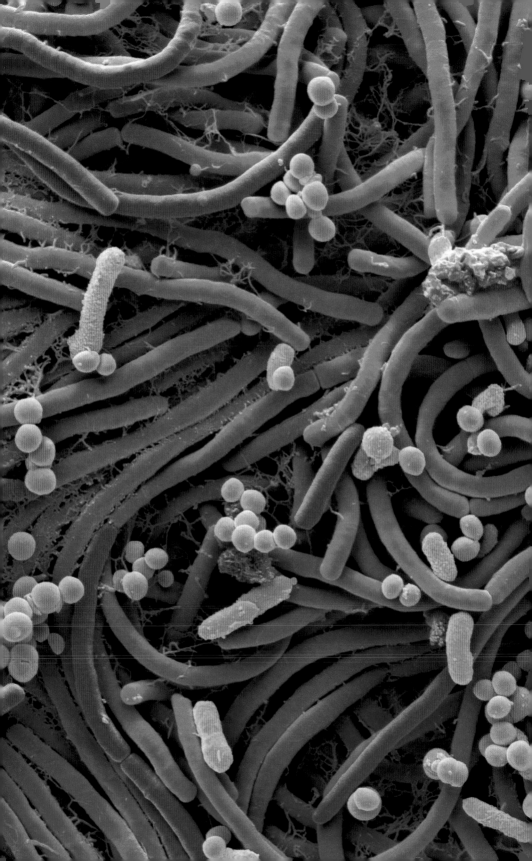

Self-Defense

Viruses, bacteria, and other tiny organisms are continually trying to get inside you and multiply, which can make you unwell. Fortunately, your body's immune system is very good at repelling these microscopic invaders.

This microscope image shows bacteria grown from finger marks on a phone screen. Tests reveal that phones have about 10 times more bacteria per square centimeter than toilet seats, including types of bacteria that cause disease.

HOW MANY
MICROBES
LIVE IN YOUR
BODY?

Your body is home to trillions of other living things that are too small to see. Called microbes or microorganisms, they live all over your skin; inside your mouth, nose, ears; and in most parts of your digestive system. Most are harmless or even helpful. However, some can make you sick if they get into the wrong part of the body. Harmful microbes are called pathogens or germs. There are also pathogens much bigger than microbes—such as worms that live in your intestines.

FAST FACTS

The largest pathogen that infects humans is the tapeworm. It can grow to 30 ft (9 m) long in a person's intestines.

Tapeworms anchor themselves inside your intestines with hooks on their head. They have no eyes, mouth, or stomach and feed by absorbing food already digested by your body.

Each blob in this handprint is a whole colony of bacteria or fungi. ·················

 WASHING YOUR HANDS HELPS STOP **GERMS** FROM SPREADING.

 CORDYCEPS IS A FUNGUS THAT INFECTS ANTS AND TAKES OVER **THEIR MINDS.**

About
**40 trillion
microbes**
live on and in
your body.

In a lab, microbes are grown on a jelly that's rich in nutrients.

This photo shows microbes grown in a lab from a person's handprint. Each spot or patch is a colony of thousands of microbes that grew from a single original cell. More than 1,000 different kinds of microbes live on human skin, feeding on grease and dead skin cells. Your hands can also pick up microbes when you touch things. If microbes infect (get into) cuts, they can multiply and cause painful sores.

HOW IT WORKS

Five main types of pathogens infect the human body. The most common of these are bacteria and viruses.

Bacteria are tiny single-celled organisms found just about everywhere on Earth.

Viruses are extremely tiny particles that can take over cells, forcing them to make more copies of the viruses.

Multicellular parasites are the largest pathogens and include worms and lice.

Fungi are fine, threadlike life forms that feed on dead or living organisms. Some fungi, such as yeasts, are single cells.

Protozoans are single-celled microbes that behave like tiny animals. The disease malaria is caused by a protozoan.

10,000 SPECIES OF MICROBES CAN LIVE ON OR IN THE HUMAN BODY.

VACCINES PROTECT YOU FROM SOME OF THE DEADLIEST PATHOGENS.

HOW SMALL IS A
BACTERIUM?

Bacterial cell

Bacteria are the most common life forms on Earth and live everywhere, including all over and inside you. The average person has more bacterial cells than human cells, but bacteria are so tiny that they make up less than 1 percent of your weight. Bacteria are too small to see with the naked eye, but you've definitely smelled them—they are responsible for the strongest and most unpleasant smells the human body produces.

Bacteria are so tiny that **hundreds** can fit on the **point of a needle.**

FAST FACTS

Bacteria live all over your skin but like dark, damp crevices best. Scientists in the US sampled 60 people's belly buttons and found 2,368 species of bacteria, most of which were new to science.

One level teaspoon of poo contains about 500 billion bacteria. Your intestines are full of bacteria that help break down food to release vitamins and other nutrients.

1 IN 6 PHONES HAVE FECAL BACTERIA ON THE SCREEN.

BACTERIA HAVE BEEN ON EARTH FOR 3.5 BILLION YEARS.

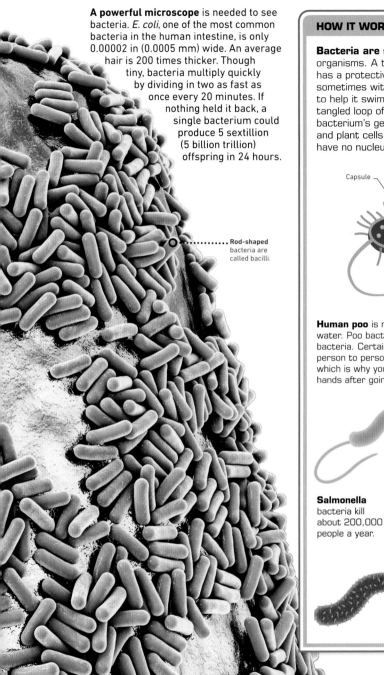

A powerful microscope is needed to see bacteria. *E. coli*, one of the most common bacteria in the human intestine, is only 0.00002 in (0.0005 mm) wide. An average hair is 200 times thicker. Though tiny, bacteria multiply quickly by dividing in two as fast as once every 20 minutes. If nothing held it back, a single bacterium could produce 5 sextillion (5 billion trillion) offspring in 24 hours.

Rod-shaped bacteria are called bacilli.

HOW IT WORKS

Bacteria are single-celled organisms. A typical bacterium has a protective outer capsule, sometimes with tiny hairs or a tail to help it swim. Inside the cell is a tangled loop of DNA carrying the bacterium's genes. Unlike animal and plant cells, bacterial cells have no nucleus.

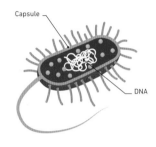

Capsule

DNA

Human poo is mostly bacteria and water. Poo bacteria are also called fecal bacteria. Certain types can spread from person to person and cause diseases, which is why you should wash your hands after going to the bathroom.

Cholera bacteria kill about 100,000 people a year.

Salmonella bacteria kill about 200,000 people a year.

Shigella bacteria kill more than 200,000 people a year.

ABOUT **6 BILLION** BACTERIA LIVE ON EACH SQUARE INCH OF YOUR SKIN.

BODY ODORS ARE OFTEN CAUSED BY BACTERIA FEEDING ON **SWEATY** SKIN.

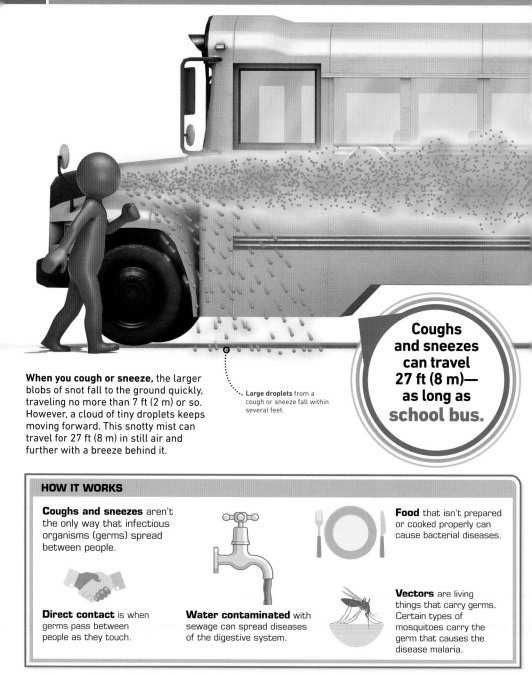

Large droplets from a cough or sneeze fall within several feet.

When you cough or sneeze, the larger blobs of snot fall to the ground quickly, traveling no more than 7 ft (2 m) or so. However, a cloud of tiny droplets keeps moving forward. This snotty mist can travel for 27 ft (8 m) in still air and further with a breeze behind it.

Coughs and sneezes can travel 27 ft (8 m)— as long as **school bus.**

HOW IT WORKS

Coughs and sneezes aren't the only way that infectious organisms (germs) spread between people.

Direct contact is when germs pass between people as they touch.

Water contaminated with sewage can spread diseases of the digestive system.

Food that isn't prepared or cooked properly can cause bacterial diseases.

Vectors are living things that carry germs. Certain types of mosquitoes carry the germ that causes the disease malaria.

SOME PEOPLE SNEEZE WHEN THEY SEE BRIGHT LIGHTS.

IT'S SAFE TO SNEEZE WITH YOUR EYES OPEN AS THEY CLOSE AUTOMATICALLY.

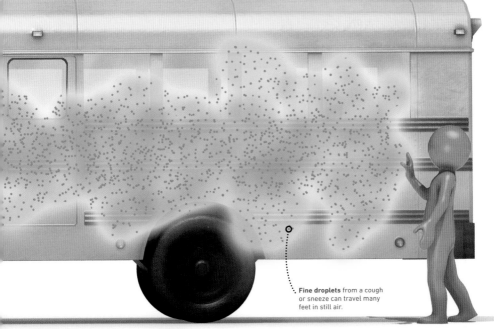

Fine droplets from a cough or sneeze can travel many feet in still air.

HOW FAR DOES
A SNEEZE
TRAVEL?

The microscopic organisms that cause diseases spread from person to person in a lot of ways, but one of their most common tricks is to make people cough and sneeze. A cough or a sneeze can send as many as 40,000 tiny droplets of snot, spit, and mucus sailing through the air, often with germs hidden inside them. Measles, mumps, chickenpox, tuberculosis, influenza, COVID-19, and the common cold all hitch a ride this way—so use a tissue!

FAST FACTS

By capturing coughs and sneezes with high-speed cameras, scientists found that the particles reach speeds of 67 mph (108 km/h) as they explode out of the nose and mouth.

108 KPH

Even ordinary speech can launch tiny droplets of fluid into the air, which another person can breathe in. However, speech spreads germs in only small numbers, making it easier for the human immune system to destroy them.

A SNEEZE ERUPTS FROM YOUR NOSE AS WELL AS YOUR MOUTH.

1 BILLION PEOPLE HAVE BEEN KILLED BY THE LUNG DISEASE TUBERCULOSIS IN THE LAST 200 YEARS.

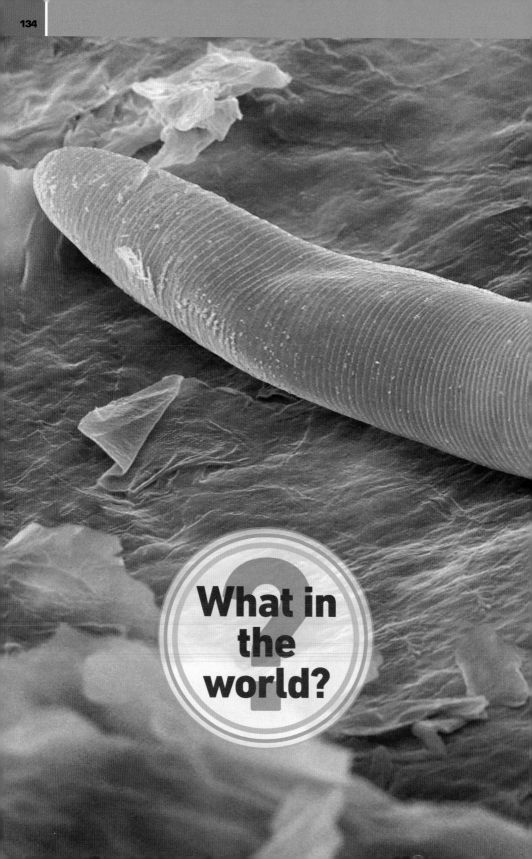

What in the world?

FOLLICLE MITE

This is a follicle mite—a worm-shaped creature less than half a millimeter long that lives in the roots of human hairs. Nearly everyone has them, and they are most common in your eyelashes and on your nose and cheeks. During the day, they stay hidden in the roots of hairs, but at night they crawl about on your face to find fresh hairs or mates. They live for only a week or so and are thought to be harmless.

HOW IT WORKS

All viruses reproduce by hijacking cells and making them produce copies of the virus.

Virus

1. The virus identifies a victim using protein molecules on its surface.

2. It invades the cell and releases its genes as DNA or RNA.

3. The viral genes instruct the cell to make copies of all the parts of the virus.

4. Millions of copies of the invading virus emerge from the cell.

Ant's foot
300 μm wide

A virus is dwarfed by objects as small as the foot of an ant or a grain of sand or salt, shown here in typical sizes. Scientists use units called micrometers (μm) to measure objects this small: 0.04 in (1 mm) = 1,000 μm. Anything smaller than about 40 μm (0.04 mm) is impossible to see with the naked eye. A coronavirus is a mere 0.1 μm across.

Grain of sand
120 μm

Grain of salt
60 μm

White blood cell
25 μm

THE **SPANISH FLU** PANDEMIC OF 1918–1920 KILLED AT LEAST **50 MILLION** PEOPLE.

COVID-19 STANDS FOR **CO**RONA**VI**RUS **D**ISEASE 20**19** (THE YEAR IT WAS DISCOVERED).

HOW SMALL IS
A VIRUS?

Viruses are so tiny that 400 million could fit inside a period. They're the smallest living things on Earth and consist of little more than a strip of genes wrapped in a protein coat. In fact, they're so small and simple that most scientists don't regard them as living. Even so, viruses are perfectly capable of reproducing. They do so by invading our cells, taking over, and forcing them to manufacture millions of copies of the virus.

FAST FACTS

If a coronavirus was scaled up to the size of a soccer ball, the human body would be as big as the moon.

Scientists estimate there are 10 nonillion (10 million trillion trillion) viruses on Earth. If you laid them all end to end, they would stretch 100 million light-years, which is 500 times greater than the diameter of the Milky Way galaxy.

A human
hair is about
1,000 times
wider than a
coronavirus.

Coronaviruses are ball-shaped and covered in proteins called spikes, which they use to attach to and enter human body cells. Inside the ball are the virus's genes, stored on a molecule called RNA (ribonucleic acid).

Human hair
120 µm wide

Pollen grain
15 µm

Dust particle
10 µm

Cough droplet
7 µm

Bacteria
2 µm

Coronavirus
0.1 µm

A SINGLE DROP OF SEAWATER CONTAINS ABOUT 10 MILLION VIRUSES.

VIRUSES CAN SURVIVE FOR 30,000 YEARS TRAPPED IN ICE.

What in the world?

VIRUSES

The red colored specks in this microscope image are viruses attacking a cell in the human body. Viruses cause some of the most common diseases to affect humans, from chickenpox and measles to COVID-19 and AIDS. They reproduce by invading our cells and hijacking them, since they have no cells of their own. The virus seen here is called human immunodeficiency virus (HIV) and causes the deadly disease AIDS (acquired immune deficiency syndrome). One reason this virus is so dangerous is that it targets the cells of the human immune system, wrecking the body's defenses.

WHY DO FEET
SMELL?

What's that cheesy odor? It might be your feet! Foot odor is perfectly normal and is caused by bacteria feeding on sweaty skin inside stuffy shoes. As you get older, other parts of your body will start making an oily kind of sweat that bacteria love, making you even smellier. If you don't want smelly feet, there's a simple solution: keep your feet dry. Skin bacteria can't thrive without moisture.

> Smelly feet get their odor from the same bacteria used for **making cheese.**

This microscope image shows foot bacteria magnified 10,000 times in size. These bacteria feed on moist, decaying skin cells between your toes and on your soles.

ON AVERAGE THERE ARE **60 TYPES OF FUNGUS** UNDER EACH TOENAIL.

YOUR **FEET** HAVE **4,000** SWEAT GLANDS PER SQUARE INCH.

FAST FACTS

Carrying flower bouquets became popular in the 15th century as a way of masking awful odors.

Mosquitoes that feed on human blood find the smell of sweaty feet attractive.

Perfumes are often used to hide natural body smells. The most expensive perfumes contain ambergris, a whiffy wax found in whale poo.

The cheesy smell of sweaty feet comes from brevibacterium, a type of bacteria used to make strong-smelling cheeses such as Wisconsin brick, raclette, and Limburger. About 1 in 10 unlucky people also have a particularly stinky kind of bacteria called kytococcus, which makes feet smell like rotten eggs.

HOW IT WORKS

Sweat is made by glands in your skin. Most sweat glands produce a watery liquid to cool the body. As you get older, special sweat glands in your armpits, groin, ear canals, eyelids, and nose also start producing an oily, smelly kind of sweat that causes body odor.

Eccrine sweat glands produce a watery sweat that cools you down.

Apocrine sweat glands produce an oily sweat that makes you smell.

YOUR LIPS HAVE NO SWEAT GLANDS.

DOGS AND **CATS** HAVE SWEAT GLANDS ONLY ON THEIR FEET.

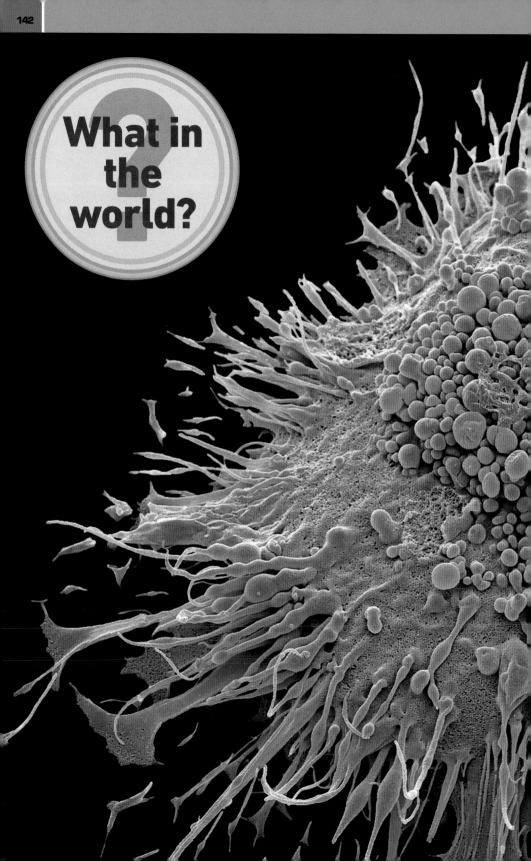

What in the world?

MACROPHAGE

An army of cells called macrophages continually patrols your body, searching for germs such as bacteria, damaged tissue, cancer cells, or any kind of dirt or debris. They move by changing shape and squeezing through the tiny gaps between the body's cells. If they find anything suspicious, they flow around it to engulf it, before killing and digesting it. A single macrophage can swallow and digest up to 100 bacteria.

Immune System Facts

BODY *BARRIERS*

It isn't easy for **germs** (pathogens) to get *inside you.* Your body has a **lot of barriers** *to trap and destroy them.*

Tears contain a substance that *splits* bacteria, killing them.

Wax produced inside your ear canal helps *clean out* dirt and germs.

Mucus is a sticky fluid that *traps* germs you swallow or inhale.

Skin forms a thick, waterproof layer that germs *can't penetrate.*

Acid produced by your stomach *kills* swallowed germs.

Saliva has chemicals that *destroy* germs in your mouth.

ATTACK AND DESTROY

If germs do **invade** your body, the cells of your **immune system** *go on the attack.* Defensive **white blood cells** *squeeze out of blood vessels* and build up where germs are found, forming pus. Many of these cells are **macrophages,** which *swallow and digest* pathogens or damaged body cells.

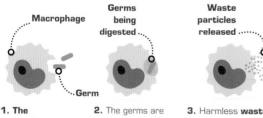

Macrophage

Germs being digested

Waste particles released

Germ

1. The macrophage *identifies* **germs** as foreign and *flows around* them.

2. The germs are *trapped* in a **bubble** and digested by **powerful chemicals.**

3. Harmless **waste** is *released* and the macrophage *continues* hunting for **invaders.**

IMMUNITY

Special white blood cells called **memory cells** *remember germs* that have infected you. If the same germs invade your body *again,* memory cells produce large quantities of defensive chemicals called **antibodies** that *kill the invaders,* giving you **immunity.** *Vaccines* give people immunity artificially. They're made from **modified germs** that are harmless but *trigger the production* of memory cells.

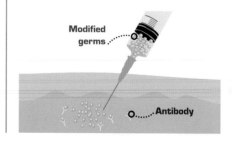

Modified germs

Antibody

THE **BLACK DEATH** AND OTHER BUBONIC PLAGUES WERE SPREAD BY FLEAS.

A **FEVER** (HIGH TEMPERATURE) MEANS YOUR BODY IS FIGHTING AN **INFECTION.**

ALLERGIES

Sometimes the human immune system **overreacts** and **attacks** *normally harmless substances* instead of germs, causing what we call an **allergy.** The affected part of the body *becomes swollen and sensitive.* A very **severe allergic reaction** can be *dangerous* as it may affect a person's **heart** or **lungs.** Here are some *common allergies.*

Animal hair

Peanuts

Pollen (hay fever)

Household dust

Insect stings

Antibiotics

EPIDEMICS

Some germs can spread quickly to **infect huge numbers of people**. When this happens, we call it an **epidemic.** If the epidemic *spreads around the world* to affect many different countries, it's a **pandemic.**

Top five pandemics

Black Death
1346-1353
75–200 million deaths

Spanish flu
1918-1920
17–100 million deaths

First bubonic plague
541-542
15–100 million deaths

HIV/AIDS
1981-present
35 million deaths

Third bubonic plague
1855-1960
12 million deaths

GRUESOME PARASITES

Parasites are small organisms that *live on or in other organisms,* feeding on their **body.** Many of the parasites that live on or in humans do little harm, but some cause **gruesome** diseases.

Botflies *lay their eggs on mosquitoes,* which leave them on a person's skin when they **bite.** *Maggots* hatch and **burrow into the bite** *to feed on flesh.*

Acanthamoeba is a single-celled soil organism that can *infect* a person from **dirty contact lenses.** *Scarring of the eye* can lead to **blindness.**

Filarial worms spread via insect bites. These tiny worms can *live in the body for years* and may cause a person's legs to *swell up* **like elephant legs.**

Guinea worms *spread in dirty water.* After living in a person's body for months, the **female worm** *breaks out through a blister* to complete her life cycle.

Hookworms can infect people who *walk barefoot* in soil that contains **human poo.** They travel *through the body* to the **intestines,** where they lay eggs.

DISEASES SPREAD BY MOSQUITOES INCLUDE MALARIA AND DENGUE FEVER.

BLOOD CELLS CALLED KILLER CELLS PROTECT YOU FROM CANCER AND VIRUSES.

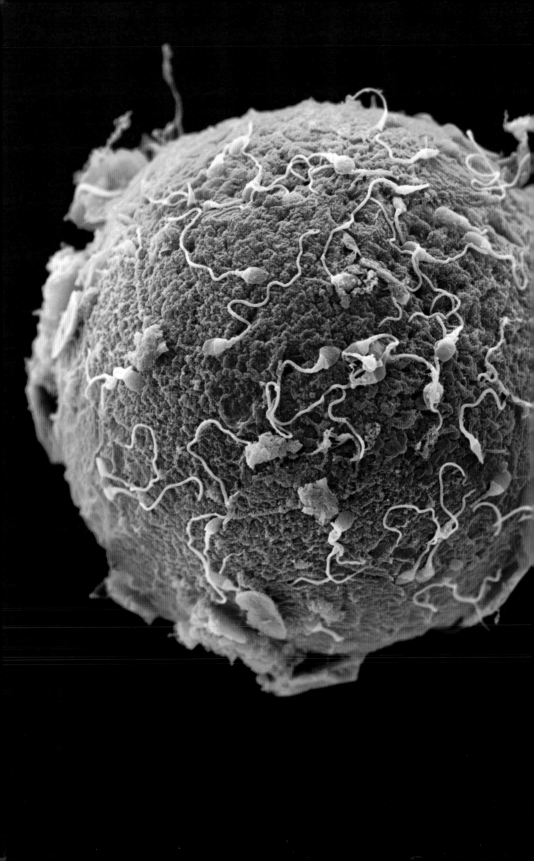

ne Cycle
Life

Your life began about nine months before you were born. At first, you were a single cell no bigger than a period, but over time you grew and developed into your complex body made of trillions of cells.

A new life begins when a sperm cell joins with an egg cell. This is called fertilization and usually takes place in a mother's body. Sperm are produced in vast numbers. Thousands race to find an egg cell and burrow into it first, but only one can succeed.

HOW BIG IS
A BABY?

The human body starts off as a single cell only a 0.004 in (0.1 mm) wide. Over the following weeks, this tiny speck of life develops into a baby with a fully functioning body of 2–3 trillion cells. Most of its organs form in the first two months, while it is smaller than your thumb and called an embryo. It spends another seven months or so growing in its mother's body before it is ready for the outside world.

HOW IT WORKS

A baby develops inside a part of the mother's body called the uterus (or womb). This muscular chamber is filled with fluid to cushion the baby against knocks and bumps. An organ called a placenta forms inside the uterus. Blood vessels from the baby flow through an umbilical cord to the placenta, where they pick up oxygen and nutrients from the mother to nourish the baby.

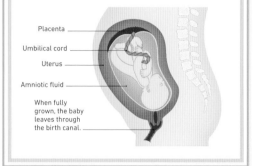

Placenta

Umbilical cord

Uterus

Amniotic fluid

When fully grown, the baby leaves through the birth canal.

At one month old, a human embryo is about the size of an **apple pip.**

At one month, an embryo is the size of an apple pip and looks a bit like a tadpole. It has a head and tail but only buds where its arms and legs will be.

At two months, the embryo is the size of a raspberry. It has arms and legs with webbed hands and feet, and its mouth, tongue, and teeth are developing.

At three months, the baby is the size of a lemon and is called a fetus rather than an embryo. It can open and close its fingers and suck its thumb.

At four months, the fetus is the size of a pear and is able to move its arms and legs. Its hair begins to grow and it can hear sounds.

At five months, the fetus is the size of a papaya and is starting to look like a baby. Its eyes can sense light and dark but are still closed.

NEWBORN BABIES SLEEP FOR UP TO 18 HOURS A DAY IN SHORT BURSTS.

ELEPHANTS HAVE THE LONGEST PREGNANCY OF ANY ANIMAL: 23 MONTHS.

FAST FACTS

Babies can taste their mother's food in the womb. They gulp amniotic fluid when they taste something sweet.

The longest human pregnancy on record lasted 375 days, which is 95 days longer than average.

375

At six months, the fetus has reached the size of a large grapefruit. It can swallow the fluid surrounding it, and its lungs practice breathing movements.

At seven months, the fetus is the size of a coconut. It can now recognize its mother's voice, but it spends most of its time sleeping and dreaming.

At eight months, the fetus is about the size of a honeydew melon and all its organs are working. It now has much less room to move about inside the uterus.

At nine months, the fetus is as big a watermelon and is ready for the outside world. Although its lungs are fully formed, they don't take their first breath of air until after the baby is born.

THE UTERUS CAN EXPAND IN VOLUME BY 500 TIMES DURING PREGNANCY.

BABY MARSUPIALS DEVELOP IN A POUCH INSTEAD OF A UTERUS.

ULTRASOUND SCAN

Ultrasound scans use the echoes of high-frequency sound waves to build pictures of structures in the body, such as an unborn baby in its mother's uterus. At only 21 weeks old, this baby is small enough to fit in one hand but can already move its arms and legs, suck its thumb, and hear.

HOW MUCH
DNA DO YOU HAVE?

DNA is an amazing molecule that stores all your genes—the instructions needed to build and run your body. There are 7 ft (2 m) of DNA in every cell nucleus in your body, giving you a total of 3.7 billion miles (6 billion km) of DNA altogether. Your genes are stored in the form of a four-letter code that runs all the way along the DNA molecule.

Your DNA could stretch to the **sun and back 20 times.**

DNA STUDIES SHOW THAT **ALL FORMS OF LIFE** ARE RELATED.

90%

90% OF YOUR DNA IS **JUNK DNA** THAT ISN'T USED FOR GENES.

HOW IT WORKS

DNA is packaged up into structures called chromosomes, which are stored in the nuclei of your cells. Human cells have 46 chromosomes, but other organisms have a different number—dog cells have 78 chromosomes, for instance, and pea cells have 14.

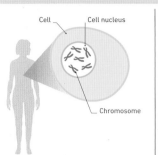

Cell

Cell nucleus

Chromosome

The four-letter code in DNA consists of four chemicals: A (adenine), C (cytosine), T (thymine), and G (guanine). A single gene may have as many as 2 million letters.

DNA is shaped like a ladder that's been twisted around. The rungs of the ladder are made of four different chemicals called bases, shown by the four colors here. The sequence of these bases forms a code, like a very long book written with only four letters. Different stretches of the code make up what we call genes, and you have about 20,000 genes altogether.

DNA is the molecule of life. Its full name is deoxyribonucleic acid.

You're nearly half banana! You share 41 percent of your DNA sequence with a banana tree, 61 percent with a fly, and 85 percent with a mouse. That's because all species are distantly related.

A printed copy of your whole set of genes—your genome—would fill 262,000 pages. That's about 175 very large (and extremely boring) books.

A HUMAN HAIR IS **40,000 TIMES WIDER** THAN A DNA MOLECULE.

THE SHAPE OF THE DNA MOLECULE IS KNOWN AS A **DOUBLE HELIX.**

Reproduction Facts

SEXUAL REPRODUCTION

Sexual reproduction involves **two parents**. They produce *female and male* **sex cells** (eggs and sperm), which join to form a cell called a **zygote**. The zygote then *divides and develops* into an **embryo**. Offspring produced sexually have a **unique mix of genes** from both parents.

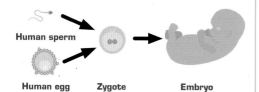

Human sperm

Human egg   Zygote   Embryo

ASEXUAL REPRODUCTION

Some animals and many plants reproduce asexually, which requires **only one parent**. The offspring from asexual reproduction are called **clones** and have **exactly the same genes** as the parent.

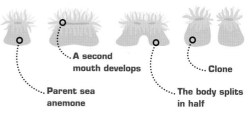

A second mouth develops

Clone

Parent sea anemone

The body splits in half

Asexual reproduction of a sea anenome

IN THE WOMB

After a human **egg** is **fertilized** by a **sperm**, it develops into a small ball of cells and implants in the wall of the mother's womb, or **uterus**, where it begins to develop into a baby.

1. A sperm and egg cell **combine to form a single cell** called a zygote.

2. The zygote **divides to produce two cells**, then four, then eight, and so on.

3. Repeated cell division produces a cluster of cells *shaped like a berry*.

4. The ball of cells **attaches to the uterus**, which feeds it. The inner cells will *form a baby*.

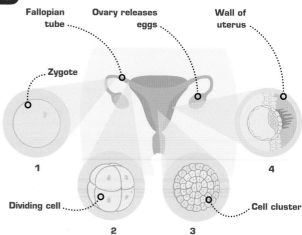

Fallopian tube   Ovary releases eggs   Wall of uterus

Zygote

1

Dividing cell   2   3   Cell cluster

4

260 **EACH MINUTE, 260 BABIES ARE BORN IN THE WORLD.**

IDENTICAL TWINS HAVE THE SAME GENES.

BOY OR GIRL?

Most of your **physical characteristics** depend on the genes your parents pass on to you. Genes are stored on **46** structures called **chromosomes**, found in every cell nucleus. Two **sex chromosomes**, called **X** and **Y**, control your sex. Females have two X chromosomes, while males have one X and one Y chromosome.

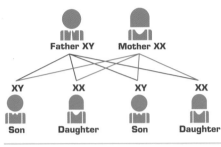

Father XY   Mother XX

XY   XX   XY   XX
Son   Daughter   Son   Daughter

GROWTH SPURTS

You grow most rapidly in your **early teens**. Your **brain** releases a **growth hormone** that makes bones lengthen, leading to a *rapid increase in height*— a **growth spurt**. *Girls* usually get their growth spurts *earlier than boys.*

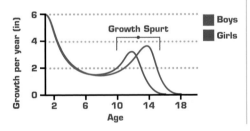

Growth per year (in)

Growth Spurt

■ Boys
■ Girls

Age

METAMORPHOSIS

Humans go through a period of change called **adolescence** between *infancy* and *adulthood*. Some animals go through a more dramatic change, known as **metamorphosis**.

Amphibian life cycle

Egg
Frogs lay their eggs in water. Each egg is protected by a thick layer of jelly.

Tadpoles
The eggs hatch into tailed young called tadpoles, with gills for breathing underwater.

Growing
The tadpoles grow legs. They lose their gills and start to gulp air at the surface.

Froglet
Front legs appear and the tail shrinks away. The young frog leaves the water.

Adult frog
Frogs breathe air and move on land, but they return to ponds to breed.

Insect life cycle

Egg
Butterflies lay their eggs on the undersides of leaves. Larvae (young insects) hatch out.

Caterpillar
A butterfly larva is called a caterpillar. The caterpillar feeds on leaves nonstop.

Growing
The caterpillar sheds its skin, or molts, several times as it grows.

Pupa
The caterpillar enters a resting stage known as a pupa. Its body slowly changes.

Adult butterfly
A winged adult emerges from the pupa. It is unable to grow any more.

GROWING A BABY

Some animals have a much **longer pregnancy** than humans. This means their babies are **well developed** at birth, which gives them the best possible chance of **survival** in the wild.

Human
Pregnancy 9 months

Giraffe
Pregnancy 15 months

Elephant
Pregnancy 22 months

MONOTREMES ARE UNUSUAL **MAMMALS** THAT **LAY EGGS** INSTEAD OF GIVING BIRTH.

A **QUEEN BEE** CAN LAY **1,500 EGGS** A DAY.

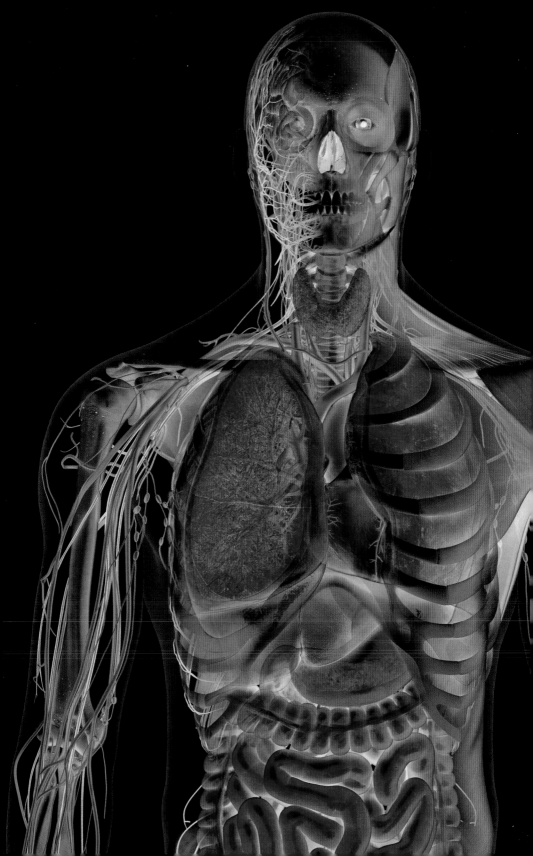

Your Operating Systems

Your body is a complex machine with many different parts, from microscopic cells to major organs such as the heart and brain. Organs team up to form body systems, cooperating to carry out difficult tasks such as digesting food or making you move.

Body systems are woven together. For instance, your muscular system is wrapped around your skeletal system, and both of these are fed by your circulatory system and controlled by your nervous system.

SKELETON

The hard bones that make up your skeleton, or skeletal system, support your body, give it shape, and help enclose and protect softer vital organs such as your brain and heart. Some bones also help generate blood cells.

Bones link together at places called joints. Most of these joints, such as the elbows and the knees, are flexible to allow movement. Other joints, such as those between the bones of the skull, are fused and immobile.

Ligament is a tissue that links bones together.

Bone marrow

Joint capsule

Synovial fluid

Synovial membrane

Compact bone

Cartilage acts like a cushion between bones.

Spongy bone

The bones in a synovial joint are tipped with cartilage. A slippery liquid called synovial fluid helps the bones slide over each other easily. Synovial joints include the shoulders, hips, knees, elbows, and the finger and toe joints.

The skull encloses and protects the brain. Together, the skull, vertebral column, and rib cage make up the axial skeleton.

The shoulder girdle has flexible joints where the arms anchor to the torso. Together, the shoulder girdle, pelvic girdle, and leg and arm bones make up the appendicular skeleton, which supports the limbs.

The rib cage surrounds and protects the lungs and heart. Muscles make the rib cage rise and fall when air is breathed in and out.

The vertebral column (spine) encloses and protects the spinal cord.

The pelvic girdle has flexible hip joints where the legs anchor to the main body.

Leg bones and arm bones are made up of a single upper bone (femur in legs, humerus in arms) that links to two lower limb bones (tibia and fibula in legs, ulna and radius in arms). The joint between them works like a hinge to flex, or bend, the limb.

Axial skeleton

Appendicular skeleton

THE FIRST **BONES TO FULLY FORM** ARE THE TINY BONES OF THE **MIDDLE EAR.**

DAMAGED **JOINTS** CAN BE REPLACED WITH **TITANIUM IMPLANTS.**

MUSCLES

Your muscular system is made up of fleshy tissues called muscles that cause movement. They do this by contracting (shortening) and pulling on other body parts. Some muscles pull on bones to move the skeleton. Other muscles squeeze the walls of vital organs, such as the beating heart.

Muscles that connect to bone are called voluntary muscles, because you have conscious control over them. The muscles of vital organs lie deeper in the body and work automatically, without you thinking about them.

The pectoral muscle is one of many chest muscles that help move the arm around the shoulder. It contracts to rotate the arm or swing the arm forward.

The belly (abdominal) muscles support the spine and upper body. They help the spine bend forward when they contract.

The arm muscles contract to pull on tendons that run through the digits to bend the fingers.

The quadriceps muscles on the front of the thigh contract to straighten the leg. The hamstring muscles on the back of the thigh contract to bend the leg at the knee.

Tendons (bands of tough tissue) link muscles to bones.

TYPES OF MUSCLES

The human body consists of three main types of muscles. Skeletal muscle moves bones. Smooth muscle squeezes hollow organs inside the body, such as the gut. Cardiac muscle keeps the heart beating.

Skeletal muscle has cylindrical cells that look stripey and do not branch.

Smooth muscle is made up of tapering, unstriped cells that do not branch.

Cardiac muscle, in the walls of the heart, has striped, branching cells.

MOST PEOPLE HAVE 42 MUSCLES IN THEIR FACE.

THE **FASTEST MUSCLES** IN THE BODY MOVE THE EYES.

BLOOD CIRCULATION

Blood carries chemicals such as oxygen, food, and waste—around your body through a network of tubes called blood vessels. It keeps moving because your heart is part of this circulatory system. The heart squeezes the blood to pump it through the vessels.

The heart pumps blood to the body's cells to supply them with food and oxygen. This oxygen-rich blood flows through arteries (shown in red). Blood flowing back to the heart carries waste produced by the cells and travels through veins (shown in blue).

BLOOD CAPILLARIES

Arteries divide into billions of microscopic capillaries that deliver oxygen and nutrients to cells. Capillaries link arteries to veins so that blood carrying waste can return to the heart.

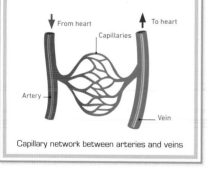

From heart

To heart

Capillaries

Artery

Vein

Capillary network between arteries and veins

The vena cava is the body's largest vein; it receives blood from smaller veins throughout the body and carries it back to the heart.

The heart has muscular chambers that beat to squeeze the blood and increase its pressure. Blood always flows from a place of high pressure to a place of low pressure.

The aorta—the largest artery in the body—delivers blood from the heart to smaller arteries that spread throughout the body.

Smaller veins carry blood containing waste products from the cells of body tissues to the vena cava.

Smaller arteries branch from the aorta to carry oxygen-rich blood to cells in different parts of the body.

BLOOD FLOW IN THE AORTA IS 500 TIMES FASTER THAN IN CAPILLARIES.

5% OF YOUR BLOOD IS IN YOUR CAPILLARIES.

LYMPHATIC SYSTEM

Every day, fluid from blood and body tissues collects in the tiny spaces between your cells. Your lymphatic system is a network of tubes that collects this fluid and carries it back to the blood as lymph. Parts of the lymphatic system also help make cells that fight infection.

The fluid that drains through the lymphatic system empties into veins. In other parts of the system, such as bone marrow and lymph nodes, your body makes and looks after infection-fighting white blood cells called lymphocytes.

Ducts empty fluid collected by the lymphatic system into the body's largest vein, the vena cava, and return it to the bloodstream.

The thymus gland is where lymphocyte cells finish developing.

The spleen, the largest lymphatic organ, helps multiply white blood cells and stores them until they are needed.

Clusters of nodes in the small intestine help protect against any harmful microbes in the food that you eat.

Lymph nodes are where lymphocytes collect and multiply. The nodes filter fluid flowing through the lymphatic system by destroying anything that might cause infection.

The marrow (not shown) inside some of your bones produces lymphocytes.

COLLECTING LYMPH

Blood is under pressure from the heart, which makes liquid squeeze out of capillaries and collect as tissue fluid. This fluid drains away into lymphatic vessels as a liquid called lymph. Valves in the vessels keep lymph flowing in one direction.

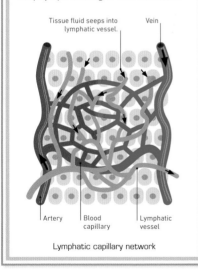

Tissue fluid seeps into lymphatic vessel.

Vein

Artery

Blood capillary

Lymphatic vessel

Lymphatic capillary network

AN ADULT CAN MAKE **1 GALLON (4 LITERS)** OF LYMPH PER DAY.

600

THE AVERAGE PERSON HAS **600 LYMPH NODES.**

DIGESTION

Your body needs nutrients to grow and fuel its cells, and the digestive system breaks down the food you eat to release these nutrients. As food moves through the digestive system, it is liquefied so that the nutrients can be absorbed into the bloodstream.

The digestive system, or gut, runs from the mouth to the anus. Its walls contain muscles for churning and moving the food, glands that release juices to help with the digestion, and blood vessels to carry away the absorbed nutrients.

The esophagus (food pipe) carries food to the stomach after swallowing.

The stomach churns food until it is liquefied and ready to be passed into the rest of the digestive system. Its glands release juices to digest protein.

The liver makes bile, which helps break down fat, and performs many other functions, such as controlling sugar levels and making poisons harmless.

The small intestine releases juices to complete digestion and absorbs most of the food's nutrients.

The large intestine absorbs water from undigested leftover material, which then leaves the body as feces (poo).

ABSORBING NUTRIENTS

The small intestine is lined with tiny, fingerlike projections called villi (singular: villus). Together, the villi provide a huge surface area for absorbing nutrients from digested food into the blood and lymph.

Digestive juices are released by glands.

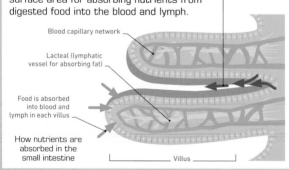

Blood capillary network

Lacteal (lymphatic vessel for absorbing fat)

Food is absorbed into blood and lymph in each villus

How nutrients are absorbed in the small intestine

Villus

WHEN YOU BURP, YOU RELEASE AIR SWALLOWED WITH FOOD.

THE SMALL INTESTINE HAS 25,000 VILLI PER SQUARE INCH (40 PER SQUARE MM).

LUNGS AND BREATHING

When you breathe using the airways and lungs of the respiratory system, oxygen from air enters your body and carbon dioxide is released. The oxygen is used by your body's cells to release energy from sugar in a process called respiration. Carbon dioxide is a waste product of respiration.

The trachea (windpipe) carries inhaled and exhaled air in and out of the respiratory system.

The lungs are packed with millions of microscopic, thin-walled air chambers called alveoli. The alveoli are surrounded by microscopic blood capillaries.

The diaphragm is a large muscle below the chest cavity that contracts and pulls downward to suck air into the lungs when breathing in. It relaxes and moves back up when breathing out.

EXCHANGING GASES

The walls of the alveoli (singular: alveolus) and blood capillaries in the lungs are each only one cell thick, allowing gases to pass easily between them.

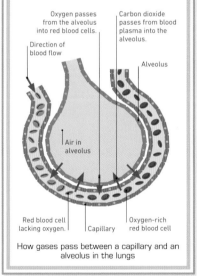

Oxygen passes from the alveolus into red blood cells.

Carbon dioxide passes from blood plasma into the alveolus.

Direction of blood flow

Alveolus

Air in alveolus

Red blood cell lacking oxygen.

Capillary

Oxygen-rich red blood cell

How gases pass between a capillary and an alveolus in the lungs

The airways leading from the mouth and nose channel air into the lungs inside the chest cavity. By branching repeatedly, the airways create a vast surface area through which oxygen can be absorbed into the bloodstream.

21 PERCENT OF THE AIR YOU BREATHE IS OXYGEN.

IN THE WOMB, A BABY'S LUNGS ARE FILLED WITH FLUID.

KIDNEYS AND BLADDER

As working cells carry out different tasks, they create toxic waste products, including a chemical called urea. The urinary system, made up of the kidneys and bladder, removes urea from the body in liquid called urine.

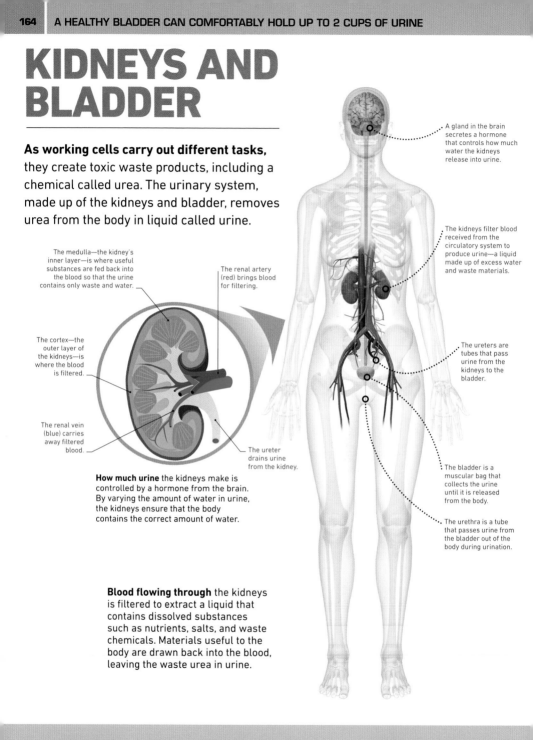

A gland in the brain secretes a hormone that controls how much water the kidneys release into urine.

The kidneys filter blood received from the circulatory system to produce urine—a liquid made up of excess water and waste materials.

The medulla—the kidney's inner layer—is where useful substances are fed back into the blood so that the urine contains only waste and water.

The renal artery (red) brings blood for filtering.

The cortex—the outer layer of the kidneys—is where the blood is filtered.

The renal vein (blue) carries away filtered blood.

The ureter drains urine from the kidney.

The ureters are tubes that pass urine from the kidneys to the bladder.

The bladder is a muscular bag that collects the urine until it is released from the body.

The urethra is a tube that passes urine from the bladder out of the body during urination.

How much urine the kidneys make is controlled by a hormone from the brain. By varying the amount of water in urine, the kidneys ensure that the body contains the correct amount of water.

Blood flowing through the kidneys is filtered to extract a liquid that contains dissolved substances such as nutrients, salts, and waste chemicals. Materials useful to the body are drawn back into the blood, leaving the waste urea in urine.

TOGETHER, THE KIDNEYS FILTER **A CUP OF LIQUID** FROM THE BLOOD EVERY MINUTE.

BEETS CAN TURN YOUR PEE RED.

REPRODUCTION

The sex organs of the reproductive system produce sex cells—the sperm and egg that join together at fertilization during sexual reproduction to make a baby. In females, the reproductive system also has parts to carry the growing baby and to feed it after it has been born.

Sex organs mature at puberty, when they start to make sex cells and when a female can become pregnant. The female organs, called ovaries, release an egg once a month. All the eggs are already present in the ovaries at birth.

The mammary glands produce and release milk to nourish a newborn baby.

The fallopian tube carries an egg from the ovary down to the womb. If sperm is present in the female's body, fertilization may happen in the fallopian tube.

The ovaries are female sex organs where female sex cells (eggs) are made.

The womb (uterus) is where a fertilized egg develops into a baby. The egg attaches to the wall of the womb, where an organ called a placenta forms to pass nourishment from the mother's blood to the growing baby.

The baby passes through the vagina (birth canal) to leave the mother's body.

Female reproductive system

MAKING SPERM

The male sex organs, the testes, make sperm continuously once puberty begins. Sperm pass to the female's reproductive system during sexual intercourse.

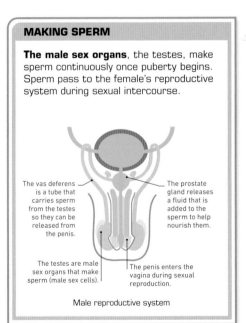

The vas deferens is a tube that carries sperm from the testes so they can be released from the penis.

The prostate gland releases a fluid that is added to the sperm to help nourish them.

The testes are male sex organs that make sperm (male sex cells).

The penis enters the vagina during sexual reproduction.

Male reproductive system

500 THE AVERAGE WOMAN RELEASES 500 **EGGS** IN HER LIFETIME.

SPERM CAN **LIVE FOR UP TO 5 DAYS** INSIDE A FEMALE'S BODY.

NERVES

Your body can respond and react quickly to its surroundings because its nervous system fires high-speed electrical signals called nerve impulses. These travel along a network of "cables" called nerves that help the sense organs communicate with the brain and muscles.

The brain is the part of the central nervous system that coordinates information and is involved in the most complex nervous processes, such as storing memories, helping us solve problems, and controlling mood and behavior.

Nerve impulses are carried from sense organs along nerves that connect to the central nervous system, which is made up of the brain and spinal cord. Other nerve impulses are carried away from the central nervous system to muscles and glands.

The spinal cord is the part of the central nervous system that receives nerve impulses from sense organs and sends nerve impulses to muscles. It also carries impulses to and from the brain.

3. At the end of the fiber, the neuron releases a chemical into the synapse to pass on the impulse.

2. A long nerve fiber called an axon carries impulses to the other end of the neuron.

1. Branching threads called dendrites receive impulses from other neurons.

4. The chemical triggers an impulse in the next neuron.

Nerves are bundles of nerve fibers that carry electrical impulses to and from the central nervous system.

The peripheral nervous system is made up of the nerves that spread out from the brain and spinal cord to every other part of the body.

The nervous system consists of long strings of cells called neurons. Tiny gaps, or synapses, separate the neurons. To pass on nerve impulses, neurons release chemicals into the synapses to bridge the gap between them.

Central nervous system

Peripheral nervous system

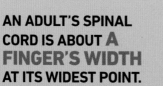

AN ADULT'S SPINAL CORD IS ABOUT A FINGER'S WIDTH AT ITS WIDEST POINT.

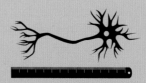

SOME NEURONS ARE MORE THAN 3 FT (1 M) LONG.

HORMONES

Your endocrine system is made up of glands that produce chemicals called hormones. The hormones travel in the blood and have powerful effects on many different organs. Unlike the nervous system, which works very quickly, the endocrine system acts over longer periods of time.

Endocrine glands are found in many different parts of the body. The hormones they release spread everywhere through the bloodstream, but each hormone will cause a response only when it reaches a particular tissue or organ.

The pituitary gland just below the brain releases many kinds of hormones that control other glands around the body. For this reason, it is known as the "master" endocrine gland.

The thyroid gland releases a hormone that controls the speed of the body's metabolism and energy release, helping regulate growth and development.

The adrenal glands, one on top of each kidney, make hormones that help regulate many vital processes, including how the body responds to stress.

The pancreas is a large gland that produces hormones to help maintain correct levels of sugar in the blood.

The sex organs (the testes in males, ovaries in females) release sex hormones that help control the development of sexual characteristics during puberty.

RELEASING HORMONES

Endocrine glands contain clusters of cells that produce hormone molecules. The molecules pass into the blood and are carried to other parts of the body.

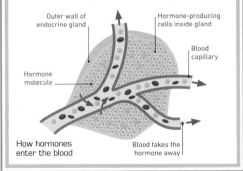

Outer wall of endocrine gland

Hormone-producing cells inside gland

Blood capillary

Hormone molecule

How hormones enter the blood

Blood takes the hormone away

 **ADRENALIN, THE "FIGHT OR FLIGHT" HORMONE, PREPARES YOUR BODY TO FACE DANGER.**

 **THE HORMONE MELATONIN CONTROLS YOUR SLEEP CYCLE.**

GLOSSARY

ABDOMEN The soft, lower part of the body below the chest (and also called the belly).

ABSORPTION The process by which digested food passes through the wall of the intestine into the blood.

ADRENALINE A hormone that prepares the body for sudden action in times of danger. Adrenaline is produced by glands on top of the kidneys.

ALLERGY Overreaction of the body's immune system to a normally harmless substance, such as pollen from flowers.

ALVEOLUS A tiny air pocket in the lungs that allows oxygen to enter the blood and carbon dioxide to leave.

AMINO ACID A simple molecule used by the body to build proteins. Proteins in food are broken down into amino acids by the digestive system.

ANTIBODY A substance made by the body that sticks to germs and marks them for destruction by white blood cells.

ANTIGEN A substance foreign to the body, such as proteins on the surface of germs.

ARTERY A blood vessel that carries blood away from the heart to the body's tissues.

AXON A long fiber that extends from a nerve cell. It carries electrical signals away from the cell.

BACTERIUM A very common type of microorganism. Some kinds of bacteria cause disease, but others help keep the body working properly.

BLOOD A liquid tissue containing several types of cells. Blood carries oxygen, salts, nutrients, minerals, and hormones around the body. It also collects waste for disposal.

BLOOD VESSEL Any tube that carries blood through the body.

BONE A strong, hard body part made chiefly of calcium minerals. There are 206 bones in an adult skeleton.

BRAIN STEM The part of the base of the brain that connects to the spinal cord.

CALCIUM A mineral used by the body to build bones and teeth. Calcium also helps muscles move.

CANINE A pointed tooth used for piercing.

CAPILLARY The smallest type of blood vessel.

CARBOHYDRATE A food group that includes sugar and starch. Carbohydrates provide energy.

CARTILAGE A tough, flexible type of tissue that helps support various parts of the body and helps joints work smoothly.

CELL The smallest living unit of the body.

CELL BODY The part of a nerve cell that contains the nucleus.

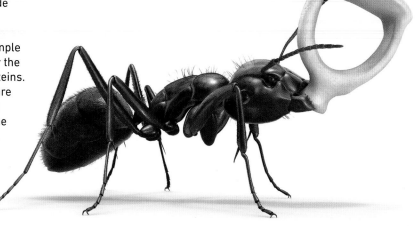

CENTRAL NERVOUS SYSTEM The brain and spinal cord together make up the central nervous system.

CEREBELLUM A small structure at the back of the brain. It helps coordinate movement and balance.

CEREBRAL CORTEX The deeply folded outer layer of the brain. It is used for thinking, memory, movement, language, attention, and processing sensory information.

CEREBRUM The main part of the brain. Its folded outer layer is called the cerebral cortex.

CHROMOSOME One of 46 packages of DNA found in the nuclei of body cells.

CILIA Microscopic hairs on the surface of cells.

CLAVICLE Also called the collarbone, a long, slender bone on the front of the shoulder.

COMPOUND A chemical consisting of different types of atoms bonded in molecules.

CONE CELLS Color-detecting cells in the retina of the eye.

CONTRACTION Shortening. Muscles move the skeleton by contracting to pull on bones.

DENDRITE A short fiber that extends from a nerve cell. It carries incoming electrical signals from other nerve cells.

DIAPHRAGM A dome-shaped sheet of muscle that separates the chest from the abdomen. It plays a key role in breathing.

DIGESTION Breaking down food into smaller molecules that the body can absorb and use.

DILATE Widen. The pupil in the eye dilates in dark conditions to let in more light.

DISEASE Any problem with the body that makes a person unwell. Diseases caused by germs are also called infectious diseases.

DNA (deoxyribonucleic acid) A long molecule found in the nuclei of cells. DNA contains coded instructions called genes that control how cells work and how the body grows and develops.

EMBRYO The name given to a developing organism in the first eight weeks after fertilization.

ENAMEL A hard-wearing material that covers the visible parts of teeth. Enamel is the hardest substance in the body.

ENDOCRINE GLAND A part of the body that makes hormones and releases them into the bloodstream.

ENZYME A substance that speeds up a chemical reaction in the body. Digestive enzymes help break down food molecules.

EPIGLOTTIS A flap of tissue that closes the trachea when you swallow food to prevent choking.

ESOPHAGUS The muscular tube through which swallowed food passes on the way to the stomach.

FAT A substance in food that provides large amounts of energy. Fats usually feel greasy or oily.

FECES Poo. Feces consist mainly of bacteria, water, and undigested food.

FEMUR (thighbone) A long bone between the hip joint and the knee joints.

FERTILIZATION The joining of a female sex cell (egg cell) and male sex cell (sperm) to make a new individual.

FETUS The name given to a baby in the uterus more than nine weeks after fertilization.

FEVER A rise in body temperature above the normal range.

GASTRIC JUICE A digestive juice made by the stomach.

GENES Instructions that control the way the body develops and works. Genes are passed on from parents to children.

GENOME The complete set of genes in a person's DNA.

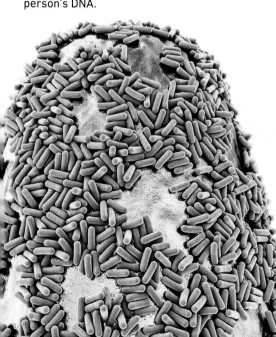

GERM (pathogen) A tiny living thing that can enter the body and make a person sick. Bacteria and viruses are types of germs.

GLAND A group of cells specialized to produce a particular substance, such as an enzyme or hormone.

GLUCOSE A simple sugar that circulates in the blood and is the main energy source for the body's cells.

HAIR FOLLICLE A pit in the skin containing the root of a hair.

HEMOGLOBIN A bright red substance in red blood cells that carries oxygen.

HORMONE A substance released into the blood by a gland in order to change how another part of the body works.

IMMUNE SYSTEM All the cells, tissues, and organs in the body that protect against disease.

INCISOR A tooth at the front of the mouth, used for cutting.

INFECTION Invasion of the body by germs, which then multiply and cause the immune system to react.

INNER EAR The fluid-filled inner part of the ear containing sensory cells that detect sound, movement, and gravity.

IRIS The colored part of the eye. Iris muscles make the pupil dilate and constrict.

JOINT A connection between two bones.

KERATIN A tough, waterproof protein found in hair, nails, and the upper layer of skin.

LARYNX (voice box) A chamber at the top of the windpipe that generates sound as you speak.

LEVER A mechanical device that swings around a fixed point, such as a door handle. The body's bones and joints work as levers.

LIGAMENT A band of very tough tissue that ties two bones together at a flexible joint.

LUBRICATION The use of a fluid between moving parts to make movement smooth.

LUNG One of two large organs used for breathing. Lungs take up most of the space in the chest.

LYMPHATIC SYSTEM A network of vessels that collects fluid from tissues, filters it for germs, and then returns it to the bloodstream.

LYMPHOCYTE A white blood cell specialized to attack a specific kind of germ. Some lymphocytes make antibodies.

MACROPHAGE A white blood cell that swallows and destroys germs, cancer cells, dead body cells, and debris in wounds.

MELANIN A dark brown pigment produced in skin, hair, and eyes that gives them their color.

MINERAL A naturally occurring solid chemical, such as salt or iron. The body needs small amounts of various minerals.

MOLAR A tooth used for grinding and crushing.

MOLECULE A group of atoms held together by very strong bonds.

MOTOR NEURON A type of nerve cell that carries outgoing signals from the central nervous system to other parts of the body.

MRI (magnetic resonance imaging) A scanning technique that uses magnetism, radio waves, and a computer to produce images of the inside of the body.

MUCUS A slippery liquid found on the inside of the nose, throat, and digestive organs.

MUSCLE A body part that contracts (gets shorter) to move bones or internal organs.

MUSCLE FIBER A muscle cell.

NASAL CAVITY A space behind the nose. Air flows through the nasal cavity when you breathe.

NERVE A bundle of nerve cells that connects the central nervous system to other parts of the body.

NERVE CELL (neuron) A cell specialized to carry high-speed electrical signals.

NERVE IMPULSE A high-speed electrical signal that travels along a nerve cell. Also called a nerve signal.

NEURON (nerve cell) A cell specialized to carry electrical signals.

NUCLEUS The control center of a cell. It contains a full set of a person's genes stored as DNA.

NUTRIENTS The basic chemicals that make up food. The body uses nutrients for energy, growth, and repair.

ORGAN A body part made of several different kinds of tissues and specialized for a particular function. The heart, stomach, and brain are all organs.

ORGANELLE A tiny structure inside a cell that carries out a specific task. The nucleus is an organelle that stores DNA.

OVARIES A pair of organs that store and release female sex cells (egg cells) in the female body.

OXYGEN A gas that is found in air and is vital for life. Oxygen is breathed in, absorbed by blood, and used by cells to release energy.

OSSICLES Three tiny bones in the middle ear that transmit sound vibrations from the eardrum to the fluid-filled inner ear.

PATHOGEN (germ) A tiny living thing that can get into the body and make a person sick. Some bacteria are pathogens.

PELVIS A large, bowl-shaped part of the skeleton formed from the hip bones and lower spine.

PERISTALSIS A wave of contraction in the muscular wall of an internal organ, such as the esophagus or intestines.

PLASMA The liquid part of blood.

PROTEINS Vital nutrients that help the body build new cells. Food such as meat, eggs, fish, and cheese are rich in proteins.

PUS A thick, yellowish liquid that forms when white blood cells build up in infected wounds.

RECEPTOR A nerve cell or part of a nerve cell that detects light, sound, movement, or some other stimulus.

RED BLOOD CELL A blood cell that picks up oxygen in the lungs and carries it around the body.

REFLEX A rapid and involuntary reaction of the nervous system, such as blinking.

RETINA A layer of light-sensitive cells in the eye. The retina captures images.

RIB CAGE The protective cage of bones around the chest formed by the ribs, spine, and other bones.

ROD CELL A light-sensitive cell in the retina. Rod cells work in dim light but don't detect colors.

SALIVA The digestive liquid produced by the mouth. Saliva helps you taste, swallow, and digest food.

SCANNING Any technique used to create images of soft tissues and organs inside the body.

SEBACEOUS GLAND A gland in the skin that produces an oily substance called sebum.

SEBUM An oily liquid that keeps hair and skin soft, flexible, and waterproof.

SENSORY RECEPTOR A nerve cell or part of a nerve cell that detects light, sound, movement, or some other stimulus.

SEX CELL A cell produced by the reproductive system. When a male and female sex cell join, a new individual forms.

SEX CHROMOSOME One of two special chromosomes that determine whether a person is male or female.

SKELETAL MUSCLE A type of muscle that is attached to the skeleton and moves the body by pulling bones.

SMOOTH MUSCLE A type of muscle found in the wall of internal organs, such as the stomach, bladder, and intestines.

SPERM Male sex cells. Sperm are made in a male's testes.

SPINAL CORD A thick cord of nerve cells that runs through the spine and connects the brain to the rest of the body.

SPINE A column of bones running down the middle of a person's back.

SUTURE A rigid joint between two bones, such as those in the skull or pelvis.

SWEAT A watery liquid produced by glands in the skin. Sweat cools down the body as it evaporates.

SYNAPSE The junction where two nerve cells meet but do not touch.

SYNOVIAL JOINT A movable joint, such as the knee or elbow, that contains a capsule of fluid for lubrication.

SYSTEM A group of organs that work together, such as the digestive system.

TASTE BUD A cluster of sensory cells in the tongue or other parts of the mouth. Taste buds sense certain molecules in food.

TENDON A band or cord of very tough tissue that connects a muscle to a bone.

TISSUE A group of cells that look and act the same. Muscle is a type of tissue.

TRACHEA (windpipe) The main airway that leads from the back of the throat to the lungs.

ULTRASOUND An imaging technique that uses the high-frequency sound to reveal structures inside the body.

URETHRA The tube that carries urine from the bladder to the outside of the body.

UTERUS (womb) A muscular organ in which a baby develops during pregnancy.

VEIN A blood vessel that carries blood back from body tissues to the heart.

VELLUS HAIR Very fine, soft hair that covers most parts of the body.

VERTEBRA One of the bones that make up the spine (backbone).

VIRUS A kind of germ that invades cells and multiplies inside them. Viruses cause the common cold, measles, and influenza.

VITAMIN An organic substance needed in very small amounts from food to keep the body healthy.

VOCAL CORDS Two small flaps of tissue in the voice box that vibrate to create the sounds of speech.

VOICE BOX (larynx) A chamber at the top of the windpipe that generates sound as you speak.

WHITE BLOOD CELL A blood cell that fights germs. White blood cells are a key part of the immune system.

WINDPIPE (trachea) The main airway leading from the throat to the lungs.

X-RAY An invisible form of radiation used to produce images of bones and teeth (or the image produced using X-rays).

INDEX

ACKNOWLEDGMENTS

The publisher would like to thank the following people for their help with making the book: Anna Pond and Lauren Quinn for design assistance, Victoria Pyke for proofreading, Sarah MacLeod for editorial assistance, Derek Harvey for consultancy, and Helen Peters for the index.

The publisher would like to thank the following for permission to reproduce their images:

(Key: a-above; b-below/bottom; c-center; f-far; l-left; r-right; t-top)

4 Getty Images: Science Photo Library / Nick Veasey (tc, tr). **Science Photo Library:** Martin Dohrn (cl); ZEPHYR (crb). **5 Alamy Stock Photo:** Science Photo Library / Steve Gschmeissner (c). **Dreamstime.com:** Akbar Solo (tc); Lev Tsimbler (tl). **Science Photo Library:** Eye of Science (tr); ZEPHYR (clb). **6-7 Getty Images:** Science Photo Library / Nick Veasey. **9 Dreamstime.com:** Alexandragl (bl). **10-11 TurboSquid:** FraP (Empire state reference)/ Dorling Kindersley/Arran Lewis.

12-13 Science Photo Library: Anne Weston, EM STP, The Francis Crick Institute. **18-19 Science Photo Library:** Martin Dohrn. **21 123RF.com:** nrey (tr). **22-23 Science Photo Library:** Power and Syred. **26 Alamy Stock Photo:** Tomasz Formanowski (r). **Getty Images / iStock:** Aaltazar (bl). **30-31 Science Photo Library:** Steve Gschmeissner. **34-35 Getty Images:** Science Photo Library / Nick Veasey (skeleton). **36-37 Alamy Stock Photo:** Science Photo Library / Nick Veasey. **40-41 Science Photo Library:** John Durham. **42 Dorling Kindersley:** Arran Lewis / Zygote (clb). **123RF. com:** Yulia Kireeva / magurok (bl). **43 Science Photo Library:** D. Roberts (br). **44-45 Dorling Kindersley:** Arran Lewis / Zygote. **46-47 Dorling Kindersley:** Arran Lewis / Zygote. **47 Dorling Kindersley:** Arran Lewis (tc, cra, crb, br). **48-49 Dorling Kindersley:** Arran Lewis / Zygote (c). **50 123RF.com:** nrey (bc). **52-53 Science Photo Library:** Martin Oeggerli. **56-57 Science Photo Library:** ZEPHYR. **60 Getty Images:** Universal Images Group / BSIP (bl). **61 Alamy Stock Photo:** Kiyoshi Takahase Segundo (tc). **66-67**

Dreamstime.com: Dawn Balaban. **70-71** Lev Tsimbler. **74-75 Dorling Kindersley:** Arran Lewis / Zygote. **76-77 Science Photo Library:** Eye of Science. **82-83 Science Photo Library:** Steve Gschmeissner. **84 Dreamstime.com:** Ildar Galeev (bc). **86-87 Science Photo Library:** Eye of Science. **90-91 Getty Images / iStock:** DmitriyKazitsyn (c). **96-97 Science Photo Library:** ZEPHYR. **98-99 Science Photo Library:** Eye of Science. **TurboSquid:** rescue3dcom (car)/ Dorling Kindersley Images: Arran Lewis. **102-103 Science Photo Library:** Steve Gschmeissner. **106-107 Dreamstime.com:** Akbar Solo. **110-111 Alamy Stock Photo:** mauritius images GmbH / Busse & Yankushev (c). **112-113 Science Photo Library:** OMIKRON. **114 Alamy Stock Photo:** Tamara Makarova (cl). **115 Shutterstock.com:** Andrey Korshenkov (cr). **116-117 Science Photo Library:** Susumu Nishinaga. **118 Dreamstime.com:** Homydesign (br); Mariia Mastepanova (bc). **118-119 Shutterstock.com:** Ruta Production (tongue). **119 Dreamstime.com:** Atlasfotoreception (bc); Gresei (bl); Chernetskaya (br). **122-123 Science**

Photo Library: Eye of Science. **125 Getty Images / iStock:** Gal_Istvan (cra). **126-127 Alamy Stock Photo:** Science Photo Library / Steve Gschmeissner. **128 Alamy Stock Photo:** Science Photo Library / Juan Gaertner (bc). **130 Dreamstime.com:** Johnpaulramirez (br). **130-131 Getty Images / iStock:** Dr_Microbe. **132-133 TurboSquid:** rescue3dcom (bus reference)/ Dorling Kindersley/ Arran Lewis. **134-135 Science Photo Library:** Power and Syred. **137 Getty Images / iStock:** ktsimage (bc). **138-139 Science Photo Library:** Steve Gschmeissner. **140 Science Photo Library:** SCIMAT (clb). **Dreamstime.com:** Aksana Kulchytskaya (bc). **141 123RF.com:** lumut (bc). **142-143 Science Photo Library:** Steve Gschmeissner. **146-147 Science Photo Library:** Eye of Science. **149 123RF.com:** khanisorn chalermchan (cla). **150-151 Science Photo Library:** Mehau Kulyk.

All other images © Dorling Kindersley
For further information see: www.dkimages.com